# Hard Corps Knowledge

## How to Succeed in

## the Marine Corps

### D. Gowans

ISBN: 1479272612
ISBN-13: 978-1479272617

# DEDICATION

Dedicated to the young men and women that continue to volunteer for the difficult and demanding duty found within the United States Marine Corps

# CONTENTS

# ACKNOWLEDGMENTS

Thank you to all the great leaders I've learned from, both seniors and juniors.

## PREFACE

This book is intended to provide useful information to first term Marines about things they can do to have a successful career in the United States Marine Corps. Ideally, this book should be purchased before going to boot camp and read a few times during the first enlistment term.

The information contained within was written because, as a senior enlisted Marine, I noticed a gap in the leadership our young Marines were receiving. Few, if any Marines at the rank of Cpl and below receive daily leadership or guidance from Marines at the E-8 and E-9 level. This is by design and due to the nature of our rank structure, but there definitely is a benefit to be had from younger Marines receiving guidance from we old, crusty enlisted Marines...

just as we are charged with assisting young Marine Officers with the leadership and guidance of his or her own platoon.

This book is my effort to provide a little bit of that guidance, based on things I've experienced and difficulties I watched younger Marines live through. The intent of this book is to provide a guideline for behavior and attitude, in order for the young Marine to have the best possible chance to excel within the Marine Corps, should he or she choose to do so. I also hope that I've provided enough information for a young Marine to look into all the opportunities the Marine Corps has to offer, for themselves, instead of relying on someone else to tell them about those opportunities.

I sincerely hope this book helps even one Marine achieve the success they hope for. Good luck, Marines!

# 1 PREPARATION: GETTING YOUR MIND RIGHT

The decision to enter the United States Marine Corps, whether going Officer or Enlisted, is a big one that should not be taken lightly. The Marine Corps just isn't for everyone. I've seen many, many smart and capable (as well as a few stupid or inept) young men and women join the Corps and have nothing but a hard time or fail outright, often resulting in punishment, brig time and/or early discharge.

Believe me; the Marine Corps is hard enough without adding to that difficulty by being a screw-up, a no-load or asking for disciplinary action through your actions or inaction. Worse still, failure, or less than 100% effort on an "individuals" part can literally result in the death of that "individual", the deaths of others, or both.

Therefore, it is imperative that if you decide to enter the Marine Corps brotherhood that you do so with the intent of giving everything you have physically, mentally and morally. This frame of mind is unnatural for most, but is an absolute necessity for your success and for the welfare of those around you.

Task number one for the "individual" that decides to enter the United States Marine Corps (that's pronounced like **core**, not like **corpse**) is to get his/her mind in the right place. That means embracing the idea that you are voluntarily giving up your individualism. You are giving up your physical freedom, your freedom of choice, your freedom of speech (to a degree) and committing yourself and your life to the Marine Corps for a definite or indefinite period of time. Failure to behave as directed, follow established regulations and fulfilling your duty on a daily basis will result in people actively making life suck for you, in an effort to correct your behavior. That's the truth, not sugar-coated crap.

Because of this commitment, serving in the Corps is especially hard for young married Marines (as well as their spouses) and exponentially harder for young married Marines with children. On top of the physical and duty related requirements, financially Marine

Corps pay is difficult to live with for a young family with children. To give you some perspective, in 2001 I was a Staff Sergeant (that's an E-6 if you're looking at a pay chart) with 11 years in service and over 3 years time in grade (time at that rank) and my family still qualified for the Women's, Infants and Children (WIC) program, a form of public assistance or "Food Stamps".

I said all this to give it to you straight, up front. I just finished a successful 20 year career in the Marines, and I'm going to tell you the truth about what goes on in the Corps and the truth about how to succeed in it on several different levels. Some people reading these first few paragraphs may already be deciding not to join the Corps. That's good. Better not to get committed to something you'll hate. Also better not to join, find out you hate it or that you can't adapt, then become a pet project for your immediate supervisors.

So, get your mind right. Get ready to sacrifice your personal desires, putting everything on hold to commit your life to the Marine Corps, because that's what it takes to really be successful.

If you're young and married, I can't recommend strongly enough that you reconsider. Your spouse will have to deal with you having a low income, you often being gone for months at a time, being uprooted every 3 years or so and moved to a new place where you don't know anyone. Finding employment for the spouse is also often difficult. If you have children, they may forget what you look like on those long deployments (no joke... it happened to me). They will be sad that you work such long hours when you are home and they will wish you could spend more time with them. It's frankly upsetting and one of the hardest things I had to deal with during my career -- denying my own children access to their father, based on a commitment I made that they had no say in.

So, if all that hasn't turned you off and made you run screaming to the Air Force recruiter, then you may be making a good choice. If the idea of suffering, being cold and miserable, unbelievably hot or routinely being assigned tasks that totally suck is appealing or humorous to you, you may be applying for the right job. I promise, there is no shortage of things that suck in the Marine Corps.

The trick is to be prepared for all those things that totally suck. Some things you'll never really be prepared for, like seeing a buddy that's right next to you get blown away. But most crappy things can be prepared for by simply accepting that those things are definitely going to happen. If you can meet challenges that suck with cheerful optimism or humor, they tend to suck a whole lot less *and* you will positively affect the Marines around you.

So, the first thing you should understand, and make sure you accept in your own mind is: The world DOES NOT revolve around you. Whether you believe this or not is irrelevant. Your upbringing is irrelevant. Other people don't exist to provide you with food, shelter, a paycheck, a job or anything else. To be successful in the Marines you must realize that the rest of the world (i.e. anyone that is not you) will act towards you as if you're just another person breathing valuable air, filling a uniform and generally taking up space. Once you understand and accept this, you are prepared to begin showing those around you that you are not just taking up space. That is your task. You want to show them, through your actions, that you are and want to be a valuable member of your unit.

Second thing you should begin to think of is yourself as a part of something much bigger. Most young American civilians tend to think of themselves as individuals and special in some way. Many people like to act out as if to prove they are special or unique. Obviously, this can be a problem if you're living in a community where you are required to maintain a minimum standard of appearance and behavior. So, forget your individualism and embrace the idea that you are a part of something much bigger. If you get your mind right and adopt these few mentality shifts, you will be well prepared to become a very important part of that much bigger something.

The last thing I'd like to bring up about your mentality is your expectations. What do you expect from a tour in the U.S. Marines? What do you think you will gain from it? I can tell you from lots of experience that you will get out of it what you put into it. Try to look at every event and every task as an opportunity to learn and become more of an asset to yourself and your unit.

Here are just a few of the opportunities that you will have access to on your first tour in the Marines:

1) Many opportunities to lead. These leadership roles will start appearing in the second week of boot camp, and will continue to be presented to you until the day you get out.

2) The chance to learn and excel in Marksmanship. In your first tour, you'll have the opportunity to shoot lots and lots of guns☺ For most, this is a definite benefit to this

career choice. Guns are really fun to shoot, and even more fun if you can shoot them really well. The good news is, the Marine Corps has one of the best Marksmanship training programs in the world. If you follow instructions, you will succeed and become a much better shot than you are now, and likely a better shot than you ever thought you could be. The Marine Corps motto regarding Marksmanship is "One Shot, One Kill", and I guarantee that you will receive world class training in how to place metal on a target with one shot.

Some of the weapons you'll get to shoot are:

A) The M16 assault rifles.

B) The M9 Barretta 9mm semi-automatic pistol.

C) The M4 assault rifle (modified M16/AR15 model).

D) The M249 **S**quad **A**utomatic **W**eapon (SAW), a 5.56mm machine gun.

E) The M240g 7.62mm machine gun.

F) The M19 automatic Grenade launcher (a machine gun that shoots grenades).

G) The M2 .50 cal machine gun.

H) The AT-4 Anti-Tank missile.

I) Grenades of many, many types including fragmentation, High Explosive, Smoke, incendiary and many other types..

… and those are just for starters. If you serve on the "ground side" there are even more opportunities. Good times will be had, I promise.

3) If you end up being good at shooting the way the Marine Corps teaches you to shoot, you may get the opportunity become a shooting coach for shooters in your unit that go to their annual marksmanship qualification. If you're selected for this duty, you'll go to a coaching course at your local rifle range. You'll learn how to teach Marines the fundamentals of Marine Corps Marksmanship on both the M16/M4 assault rifles and the 9mm pistol.

Usually you'll end up doing this duty a few times a year. For those that love shooting, this duty can be particularly gratifying as you'll have tons of opportunity to help your fellow Marines become better marksmen.

4) Good shooters also often get the opportunity to attempt to qualify for the Marine Corps Shooting Team. This opportunity comes around every year. If you're interested in this, ask your Non-Commissioned Officer In Charge (NCOIC) and he/she should be able to find out when the next one comes up. If your NCOIC has no idea, find a buddy that's an Armorer (a guy that works in the Armory) or a Rifle Range Coach and they should be able to get that information for you.

5) If you're an infantryman and a good shot, you may be given the opportunity to attend Sniper School. This school is VERY mentally and physically challenging, so if you get the chance, be prepared.

6) You'll also have the opportunity for early promotions. These are more commonly known in the Corps as "Meritorious Promotions". Meritorious Promotion opportunities will appear in boot camp and continue to be available to you through the rank of Staff Sergeant. Most units in the Marine Corps (at the Battalion and Squadron levels) are delegated quarterly meritorious quotas. The way this works is, the Commandant of the Marine Corps (CMC) authorizes a certain amount of meritorious promotions each quarter. He divvies up and delegates these quotas down through the major units. Each Battalion or Squadron ends up with one or two of these quotas for Sergeant, Corporal and Lance Corporal each quarter. Often, combat units receive a few more than non-combat units, for obvious reasons.

Anyway, each quarter these units will hold a "Meritorious Board" during which deserving young Marines are submitted to the unit Sergeant Major as nominees for the promotion. The Sergeant Major usually has a few senior enlisted Marines assist him in reviewing the service records of these Marines, then they run them through an    evaluation process. This process usually consists of at least a "board" during which    each Marine walks into a sealed room with the Sergeant Major and his senior enlisted    assistants. While in the room the Marines are evaluated on many things including    their behavior, their knowledge and their appearance. At the end of the board, the    winner for each rank is usually announced, and the winners are promoted to their new ranks on the second day of the following month.

Many units choose to run an enhanced board process in which the Sergeant Major has these Marines run a Physical Fitness Test (PFT), conduct ceremonial drill (commanding a marching platoon), a uniform inspection and sometimes a "Wall Locker" inspection (an inspection of all uniform items at one time), all before standing in front of the actual Sergeant Majors board.

Meritorious promotion to Staff Sergeant and Gunnery Sergeant come along only once a year, and there is usually only one promotion slot for each Division and Air Wing, so competition for those two are exceptionally tight. You really have to look good, both in person and on paper to win either of these two.

7) You'll also have opportunities to become a Commissioned Officer. There are several programs available to help enlisted Marines become officers. Most of these programs require the enlisted Marine to already have a college degree. One of them allows for the meritorious commissioning of enlisted Marines before they have a degree (Currently called Meritorious Commissioning Program or MCP), but if that program is used there is a set amount of time, or deadline, within which you have to complete your degree. Each year the Marine Corps selects highly qualified applicants to these various programs. All of these programs also really encourage applications from "minority" and female Marines.

When it comes time to look into these programs for yourself, the units "Career Planner" or "Career Retention Specialist" (the CRS and career planner are the same person, just a different name) should be able to help you move in the right direction. I strongly encourage you to look up each program's requirements for yourself. That means opening the applicable Marine Corps publication yourself and thoroughly reading each program's eligibility criteria and application requirements.

8) Deployments are always available. Just ask your NCOIC. Tell him/her that you'd like to go on a deployment and that you want to be the "go-to" guy when the next one comes up. The catch is, you better be ready to go! Have your personal life in order and everything arranged so that you can manage to be in some third-world country with no contact to the United States for a year or so. Being ready to go means that your personal life is stable, you're a class 2 or better with Dental, all your shots are up to

date and your will has been prepared (base legal will do this for you).

In my opinion, you should always have a "Sea bag" packed and ready to go. Marines are supposed to be deployable with very little notice, so I suggest <u>always</u> being as prepared as reasonably possible. Obviously, you can't be 100% ready all the time, but you should always be as ready as possible, perhaps 85% ready at any given time with just some loose ends to tie up before leaving.

9) Corporals Course and Sergeants course are available to those Marines of each rank. Over the years, training requirements for promotion have increased dramatically. Just a few years ago the Marine Corps only had an "NCO Course" that you would go to when you became an NCO. Later, the Sergeants course, Staff Sergeants course, Gunnery Sergeants course and the E-8 Seminar were developed and all considered "nice-to-haves" that would help to make you more competitive for promotion. More

recently we've seen the development of a Corporal's Course and even a Lance Corporals Course at some local major commands. Things have changed! These are now ALL required for promotion, except for the Lance Corporal course. Criteria for promotion will continue to evolve long after the day this book is published, so find out what the requirements are for you now, and then get them done as early as possible so you don't have to worry about it.

Here's how the Leadership schools work: When you pick up rank, you go to the school for that rank as soon as possible. So, you get promoted to Corporal on June 1st... later that day you should be talking to your boss (NCO, or Staff NCO) about the possibility of getting out to the next available Corporals course. Same goes for all the other courses. Get promoted then get to the course.

Later in your career promotions start to work differently. For Staff Sergeant (SSgt) and above there is an annual selection board. This means that all eligible Marines throughout the Marine Corps are evaluated by a group of senior Marines assigned by the Commandant of the Marine Corps. This senior group, also known as the "promotion board", reviews the service records of all eligible Marines, then votes on who gets promoted. There is a promotion board for each rank from SSgt to Sergeant Major (SgtMaj) and Master Gunnery Sergeant (MGySgt). So, in the case of the SSgt board, all Sergeants that are eligible for promotion to SSgt get looked at and evaluated by this board.

Once a Marine is "selected" for promotion to the next rank, they will have to wait a while before actually being promoted, which I'll talk more about later. But during this lag time while awaiting promotion, you are actually already eligible to attend the Leadership school of the next rank! If you have the opportunity to go during this time, DO IT! You'll thank yourself later.

10) Depending on your job, or Military Occupational Specialty (MOS), you may be presented with the opportunity to attend additional or advanced MOS schools. The best advice I can give you, regardless of your MOS is, GO TO THE SCHOOL! Don't ever, ever pass up an opportunity for additional training. It only makes you more valuable, more competent and more of a "Go-to" Marine.

11) Everybody loves "Recon". Another opportunity that occasionally pops up is Recon try-outs. Recon is short for Reconnaissance Marine. A Recon Marine is generally an infantry Marine that is in a special ground unit established to collect information. These guys get some really cool training, like jump school (parachuting), SCUBA school and other things. This job/MOS is a gateway position for the Marine Corps' elite special warfare units known as "Force Recon". Force Recon in the Marines is like the SEALs in the Navy, the Rangers in the Army or the Air Force "Special Tactics" guys. Of course, I think Force

Recon would crush most of these other Special Operations types, but I'm biased.

Sometimes they open Recon to MOS's outside of the infantry field – I saw it only one time during my 20 years. If that happens again and you want to jump on it, don't hesitate.

Anyway, the Recon try-outs are pretty brutal. I highly recommend ensuring that you are in the best shape of your life before attempting a Recon try-out. The try-out procedures have changed several times over the years and I'm sure those changes will continue, but you can expect at least one full day of extremely difficult physical activity. An example of one I saw (but chose not to participate in) went something like this:

- 0500 (that's 5:00am), Start of a Physical Fitness Test (PFT) which includes maximum pull-ups, maximum sit-ups and a 3 mile run. 1st class score required to continue.

- 0600, Start of Obstacle Course run consisting of 3 times through the obstacle course, back to back. This was a timed event with a minimum time required to continue.

- 0700, Start of Swim Qualification from 4th class to Water Survival Qualified (WSQ). This is essentially 5 swim qualifications back to back, each one harder than the last.

- 1000, Start of a 15 mile "hump" with an 80 lb pack. This is a 15 mile hike with a lot of weight on your back. Of course this was a timed event and if you failed to make the cut-off, you were out.

- 1500, PFT #2, 1st class score required to continue.

- 1600, pool exercise period consisting of swimming, suspended leg lifts, lots of push-ups, etc.

- Finally around 1700 they wrapped things up. Starting with the hump and every event afterward, the Recon evaluation team members were chasing the candidates through each event, yelling at them, trying to get inside their heads and make

them quit.

This Recon Indoctrination process (Indoc) was just to see

if those applicants had the guts/will to keep going even

after their bodies had been abused all day. These

procedures have changed several times over the years, but

you can be sure that if you try out for Recon, your mettle

will be tested.


Towards the end of your first tour, other opportunities will start

to pop up. By the time you've done 4 years of active duty, you'll most

likely be a Non-commissioned Officer (NCO), probably a Corporal.

Most enlistment contracts these days are either 4 or 6 years. As an

NCO you will be eligible for special duties like Recruiting, Marine

Security Guard duty, Drill Instructor duty or School of Infantry

instructor. All these duties are tough, but they have their benefits too.

If you're planning a career in the Marines and have a desire to ever be

a First Sergeant (1stSgt) or Sergeant Major (SgtMaj), doing one of

these special duties is critical to making yourself competitive later in

your career. If you want to be a career Marine, get one of these done.

Just do it. The earlier in your career you do it, the easier it will be on you and the better off you'll be.

Lastly, as your first tour comes to an end, you'll start hearing about re-enlistment opportunities and incentives. Each Division and Air Wing sometimes offers a few seats in the Army Jump School, The Pathfinder School, or Marine Scuba School as an incentive to re-enlist and remain in your MOS. These school seats are rare because usually there are very few seats allotted to incentive programs. So, if you get the chance to go to one of these and want to re-up (re-enlist), take it.

There are also always "Lat-move" opportunities. That means that after you complete your first tour, you do a "Lateral Move" into a completely different MOS. This is a great opportunity to experience a different side of the Marine Corps. I did one of these myself after my first tour. I was a Field Radio Operator in 1994. I was in Okinawa at the time and since we didn't have the internet on Okinawa back then I really had no way to even look for a job until I got back to the states and discharged from the Corps. Well, I didn't like the sound of looking for a job after I'd been released from my current job, so I decided to try re-enlisting for a different MOS.

After my first tour I did a lat-move and became an Air Traffic Controller. I'll tell you, it wasn't easy going from a ground-side MOS to an Air Wing MOS. You wouldn't think it would be any big deal, but it really was a major adjustment. So consider carefully your choices. For more information on lateral moves you can go see your Career Planner (Now called the Career Retention Specialist... I wonder if they changed the name because we always referred to them as "Career Jammers"). They are the ones responsible for helping Marines Re-enlist, whether it be in their current MOS or a Lat-move into a new MOS. They have all the information and MOS eligibility requirements and will help you make an intelligent decision regarding your career. Note: If you think you might want to become an Air Traffic Controller, talk to one first. I recommend talking to one that Lat-moved into the job and preferably a senior one (Gunnery Sergeant or higher) that has been around the block a few times.

As you can see, there are a ridiculous amount of opportunities, even in your first years in the Corps, to go out and do things that are a little outside the norm. Take advantage of them. They give you invaluable experience and generally make you a better Marine. I'm not saying you should spend all your time doing these extra things. You must be extremely proficient in your main job or MOS, otherwise someone else will have to pull your weight, and that's bull crap! Get good at your job, then go out and experience all the Corps has to offer. This is a recipe for a very successful career and a GREAT time!

## 2 SELECTING YOUR JOB

If you're reading this you're most likely already a Marine, but if you haven't yet gone to Boot Camp, you'll find this useful. Your recruiter will guide you through the enlistment process. Whether you want to ship out to boot camp in 2 days or 10 months, they will set everything up for you. All you have to do is show up when they tell you to show up.

The first order of business is to get you to take the Armed Services Vocational Aptitude Battery (ASVAB). This is a test that is usually given at the Military Entrance Processing Stations (MEPS). It will take a few hours to complete. It is in your best interest to do as good as you possibly can on this test. Your results on this test will dictate which jobs will be available to you when you join the Corps. If you do well enough, you'll be eligible for any job in the Marine

Corps. That's the best possible scenario. You'd rather pick any job you want, right?

Even if you do really well on the ASVAB and are eligible for any job in the Marine Corps, you still may be restricted in some jobs due to no fault of your own. The Marine Corps has a very specific number of positions at each rank within each MOS. That means, sometimes a particular MOS may be full. If an MOS is full, they will not let anyone else into the MOS until someone gets out, gets promoted or becomes a casualty to make room for more entry-level Marines. This is pretty common. At any given time, the odds are that some MOS's will be full and not available for entry. This also becomes a factor when re-enlisting. I've seen good Marines that wanted to re-enlist in their MOS, but could not because there just wasn't any more space for them (often called "boat spaces"). The only options for a Marine in this position are to Lat-move to a different MOS, get out and try to re-enter, get out and become a Marine Reservist, or just get out.

Jobs can also be selected by generality. That means instead of picking a specific job, you could pick a general field of jobs and the Marine Corps will put you into one of those jobs based both on their needs at the time and your abilities revealed in the ASVAB test. For example, you're not sure what job you want. You'd like to be part of the aviation community but you don't necessarily what to fly. You could select the general MOS field of Aviation Command and Control (the 7200 field). The Marine Corps would then send you to the school within that general field of specialties that they need more entry-level people in at that time. You could end up as a Direct Air Support Coordinator, as an Air Traffic Controller, as a Tactical Air Operations Center Marine or a number of other jobs. These jobs are related, but often completely different. If you have the opportunity, ask someone about these jobs before committing to a general field enlistment.

If you have absolutely no idea what you want to do, but just want to sign up and get to boot camp, you could also elect to join up on an "Open Contract". That means that once you graduate boot camp, the Marine Corps will put you in whatever job that 1) your ASVAB score makes you eligible for, and 2) they need entry-level Marines in at that time. If you like surprises, this might be the way to go!

If you don't necessarily want to make the Marine Corps a career, I recommend choosing a job that has some potential for employment once you exit the Marine Corps. Some examples of this might be: Communications Technician, Computer Technician, Air Traffic Controller, Aircraft Mechanic, Motor Transport Mechanic, HVAC Technician, Heavy Equipment Operator, etc. If you're interested in the medical field, you'll need to join another service. The Marines don't have doctors, dentists or nurses. Our medical staff is provided to us by the Navy.

Jobs like Infantry and Reconnaissance Marine don't translate to very many employment opportunities on the outside the Marine Corps, other than security and maybe law enforcement.

Once you've selected your job, make sure that the job you selected is written in your enlistment contract. This contract is a legally binding document. If your recruiter tells you that you can be an aircraft mechanic and your enlistment contract says you're enlisting to be a cook, guess what you'll be doing for the next 4 to 6 years… I'll take a ham & cheese omelet please.

Be smart. Read your contract. Make sure you know what you're getting in to and don't let anyone push you into something you don't want.

After you get to Boot Camp, you will be exposed to other testing. One of these is the Defense Language Aptitude Battery (DLAB). This test is designed to evaluate your aptitude for foreign languages. If you already know a foreign language, you'll be a step ahead. If you do well on these tests, a whole new set of job opportunities will open to you. Most are in the intelligence field. To take advantage of these types of jobs, you'll need to pass an exhaustive background check to obtain a pretty high security clearance.

Regardless of what you signed up for with your recruiter, you may be given the chance to be trained for one of these special jobs if you do well on these tests and if you have favorable background check results.

That's it for entry-level jobs in the Marines. There are a few other jobs that you may gain access to later. For example, Explosive Ordnance Disposal (EOD) is a job that is only available to Sgts and above, therefore you can only Lat-move into this job. This is a very dangerous job that requires technical expertise and serious maturity. It's definitely not for everyone and should only be entertained by those willing to be around potentially unstable explosives on a daily basis. There are other jobs available only to seasoned Marines. For a list of these that are currently available, speak with your Career Retention Specialist, NCOIC or 1stSgt.

Whatever you end up doing, don't be upset with your recruiter if you don't like your job. Your test results dictated your eligibility. You selected your job or field from that eligibility. You sign the contract that had that MOS or field written on it. If you don't like your job, chalk it up as a mistake, be the best Marine you can be and re-read all the other opportunities I listed in Chapter 1.

# 3 WHAT TO EXPECT DURING THE FIRST 6 MONTHS

Boot Camp is also known as Basic Training. In the Marines it is approximately 13 weeks long and is followed by about 4 weeks of Marine Combat Training (MCT) unless you're an Infantry Marine. After MCT, Marines generally go in different directions to each of their respective MOS schools.

Marine Boot Camp is designed to teach you the most basic information and standards of behavior that are required to be a Marine. I emphasize the word BASIC here, because you're learning the ropes from scratch. Your purpose there is to listen, learn and do exactly what you are told to do.

I've also heard boot camp described as "90% mental, 10% physical", and I believe that to be true. If you follow direction and do what you're supposed to do, you'll make it to the end 99.99% of the time.

The key to Marine Corps Boot Camp is to do everything with a high sense of urgency, no matter what the task. It doesn't matter if you're field stripping an M-16, running the Obstacle Course (O-Course) or making a head call (going to the bathroom). Everything you do must be done quickly and thoroughly. If you fail to do even the simplest thing with urgency and correctly, you will become the focus of attention of one or more Drill Instructors (DI's). And yes, you'll have more than one drill instructor. In fact, you haven't lived until you've had five drill instructors surrounding you and yelling with their noses an inch from your head. A good strategy in Boot Camp is to put forth maximum effort and try **not** to draw undesirable attention to yourself. By undesirable attention, I mean extra guidance from a Drill Instructor.

The whole Boot Camp experience is designed to break you down and then build you into first a cohesive team member and then a leader. The idea is to remove individualism from each recruit, then build them into a military minded man or woman that can function effectively as a member of the unit or the group. That's essentially it.

Sure, you do a lot of marching, shooting guns, exercise and hiking; and these are all essential functions of a Marine. But, every task is designed to make you capable of functioning as a team member as well as a warrior and leader.

Boot camp is broken up into several phases. As I write this, boot camp consists of three phases plus the MCT as a fourth-phase of training. In the first phase you'll learn general military and Marine Corps knowledge. In the second phase you'll learn marksmanship and field skills. In the third phase you'll learn more refined general military skills, and then put everything together becoming an effective, military minded, basic Marine.

During the first week of boot camp, you'll find yourself in the "receiving" barracks. "Receiving" is a company that administratively handles incoming recruits. New recruits spend the first week getting clothing and equipment, testing, administratively processing and generally getting shown "the ropes" of boot camp.

Perhaps the most terrifying moments occur when you're arriving, getting off the bus, and stepping on those famous yellow footprints. It still happens the way it has happened for decades, the bus pulls up to the receiving building, the door opens, a drill instructor with the Smokey Bear hat (Campaign Cover) steps onto the bus and starts barking at everyone. This is where the fun starts. Everyone gets bum-rushed off the bus and onto yellow footprints in front of the building. After receiving a quick brief they start in-processing all the new recruits.

In processing is a great time! You take care of some administrative paperwork, get medical examinations and shots, you are issued uniforms and personal clothing items, you get a nice thorough haircut, then you're taken to your first barracks room (a squad bay) where the drill instructor will show you how to properly make your first "rack". This is where I had one on my most memorable experiences: I made a head call in the receiving barracks immediately after receiving my haircut. After relieving myself I went to wash my hands and was horrified to see a fleshy-headed mutant staring back at me from the mirror! Until that moment, I never realized how much I resembled Yoda from the Star Wars movies. Horrifying.

Anyway, after your "receiving" week, your platoon will be "picked up". Pickup day is when your permanent drill instructors come to the receiving barracks, pick you up and March you to your battalion/company barracks. Once you arrive at the permanent barracks usually your senior drill instructor will be there waiting for you. Your senior drill instructor will then address the platoon and introduce his team of junior drill instructors that will assist him in training you. Once all the drill instructors are introduced, all hell breaks loose. All the drill instructors go absolutely ballistic, and the next several days are spent with their collective feet knee-deep in everyone's butts until your batch of new recruits can begin to get a grip on Marine Corps life.

As I said before, boot camp is broken up into several phases. In the first phase you'll learn general military and Marine Corps knowledge. This is where you learn all the Marine jargon, the rank structure, the basics of marching, and lots of classroom training that will teach you the things you need to know. Another word of advice: Don't be the smart guy that falls asleep during a period of instruction.

In the second phase you'll learn marksmanship and field skills. You'll actually do your first rifle qualification in the second phase as well as your first "conditioning hike", and learning how to live outside... a much more anal-retentive form of camping. If you're a camper and think you know how to live outside, you're most likely missing a few bits of information, so you'll still want to pay attention.

In the third phase you'll have more classroom instruction, the marching will become second nature, your platoon will begin to sound and look like a disciplined group of steely-eyed killers.

I recent years, they have added "the crucible" to the basic training process. This takes place near the end of boot camp. You'll spend 3 glorious days and nights deprived of food and sleep, participating in team-building exercises and mock combat scenarios. At the end they'll have a ceremony in which they award you your first Eagle, Globe and Anchor (the Marine Corps emblem). At this moment, you become a Marine and you remain one for the rest of your life.

Once you graduate boot camp, you'll most likely be granted 10 days of leave to go home and see your family. Enjoy the break and, for god sake, don't do anything stupid! Making little mistakes like getting a DUI/DWI, stealing, or doing drugs, while merely a significant inconvenience in the civilian world, could cost you not just your career in the Marines but also your freedom.

You could very easily find yourself in the brig (Marine/Navy jail) for an extended stay if you break the regulations of the uniform Code of Military Justice (UCMJ). Adultery, solicitation of prostitutes and drinking under age are also severely dealt with in the Marines because they violate the UCMJ. Even if you're at the "Bunny Ranch" near Las Vegas where prostitution is legal or drinking in Tijuana Mexico (which last time I checked was "Off Limits" to Marines) where there is no drinking age, you still can't do it, because the UCMJ says so. If you're wondering why the UCMJ says so, it's usually because someone (usually more than one someone) has already done something like that and created a very inconvenient mess for everyone. Consequences are even tougher over seas. When you get busted for violating laws in a foreign country, you create an international incident. You don't want to create an international incident…. Trust me!

After your boot camp leave, you'll be expected to report in to MCT (unless you're infantry) **prior to** the reporting date and time on your orders. Don't ever report in for duty late… ever, ever, ever! If, for some reason you can't make it on time, at the very least call the office you're suppose to report in to and tell them why you won't be there on time. There will always be contact information to your next duty station on your travel orders. Make sure you call them if you have any problems, including accidents and injuries requiring hospitalization.

At MCT you will receive more detailed training on infantry operations and weapons systems. Every Marine gets this training because "Every Marine is a Rifleman". This is something that became glaringly apparent during the Korean War, when Marine and Army units found them-selves surround by Chinese troops that outnumbered them 10 to 1. The Marines were able to fight their way out of that mess because even their cooks and administrative specialists learn how to shoot and hit a target with a single bullet. If that time ever comes for you, you'll want to go down fighting, right?

Infantry Marines don't go to MCT. Instead, they go to the School of Infantry (SOI). SOI teaches the same skills that MCT does, just a little more in depth. SOI is the formal basic "A" school for an Infantry Marine.

After MCT, Marines are given new orders to their formal school. This is the school they go to that teaches them the basics of performing their main job in the Marine Corps. Notice that all these schools and training locations teach "the basics" of each job. That's because when you actually get out to the "Fleet" and start doing your job for real, you'll find out that there is far more to learn about both your job and the Marine Corps. The last thing you want to do is show up at your first duty station acting like you know everything there is to know. You don't! If you think you do, you are in for a rude awakening. I did 20+ years in the Corps and I was learning things until the day I got out. It's good to be confident, but stay humble or someone will humble you, I promise.

From my experience, most young Marines seem to have trouble in either MOS school or at their first duty station after MOS school. I'll talk about ways to stay out of trouble in both places in the next chapter.

## 4 BEING SUCCESSFUL IN MOS SCHOOL

Many young Marines get out of Boot Camp and MCT with a grand idea of how much different "the fleet" is and how they'll be "treated like an adult" more-so than they were in Boot Camp. That is true to some degree, but I have often seen this attitude lead new Marines into thinking they can behave like a lunatic without suffering the consequences. The key component to being "treated like an adult" is having the maturity to act like an adult. That means being able to resist doing things that will result in trouble, being able to accurately estimate the ramifications of your actions and being mature enough to choose NOT to do something that has a high likelihood of backfiring on you.

The truth is, once you get to your MOS school or become the new guy in your first fleet unit, you are essentially under a microscope. In these situations your direct and indirect supervisors are both watching you very closely. They are looking for signs of maturity, intelligence and ability. If you show them that you are mature, smart and capable, they will begin giving you opportunities to live up to that potential. This is how they begin to know you and understand your capabilities. What you do and how you do it will tell them everything about you.

Unfortunately this time of increased freedom sometimes leads to temptations that some find irresistible. For example, you're no longer living in a squad-bay or having drill instructors or troop handlers tell you when to go to bed and when to get up. It's on you to get the rest you need and get up at a time that will allow you to show up when and where you are suppose to show up the next day. Many young Marines find the temptation to go out at night and drink with their friends too tempting to pass up. So they go out and get drunk.

The first thing that happens when you get drunk is your judgment becomes severely impaired. Next thing you know, you're drinking way more than you intended to. You start bar hopping, then someone wants to go 5 miles down the road to a "gentlemen's" club. You all pile into your car and you, already drunk, drive everyone to the "titty bar" only to find out there's a 10 dollar cover charge. Irritated, everyone pays the $10 to get in, only to find out that it's amateur male stripper night. You and all your buddies get pissed off and demand a refund. The bouncers get involved, then the whole place gets cleared out when the bartender starts hosing the place down with his can of Anti-Bear Pepper Spray. You and all your buddies jump in your car and take off trying to get away before the cops show up. 2 miles away, you get pulled over and charged with Driving Under the Influence (DUI). While you're being arrested, one of your buddies gets out and starts puking in the slow lane. Then another buddy gets out, walks up to the nearest structure and starts pissing on the side of the building. The cop calls and ambulance for the puker and starts arresting the pisser for public "exposure". Then the owner of the structure happens to come out. It turns out that the structure your buddy chose to piss on was the side door of a 1stSgt's house, and he's not happy. See how things can go downhill? And yes, all that actually happened to young Marines I know.

This may sound like a movie script to you, but shit like this happens routinely to young Marines because the first thing to be "shit-canned" when you're drinking is your judgment. No joke. I've seen it over and over again. All it takes are a few drinks and one bad decision to start this little snow ball rolling down the hill. Once you've made a few bad decisions in a row, it's too late to stop the mess you're creating from unfolding. Just try not to be a dumb-ass.

Here's the secret to your success: Focus your efforts on your Marine duties and education. When it comes time to play or relax, do so responsibly. Go to the base pool for a few hours. Work out at the gym. Go to the beach. Go fishing. Go bowling. Go Scuba diving... whatever. Just do it without drinking. The idea is to have fun, reduce stress and bond with your buddies. If you can't have fun without drinking, you should probably get some help. If you're drinking under the age of 21, sooner or later you're going to get involuntary help, and that is the most painful kind of help to get, for sure!

So you get the point, right? Drinking = bad decisions = more bad decisions = unrecoverable cluster-fuck that could easily end in you spending several months in the brig before you get a nice dishonorable discharge, permanently removing your right to vote or hold a government job. You don't need that crap, do you? You don't need to drink to have fun. You don't have to go out late at night to have fun. I once heard a Marine leader say, "Nothing good happens after 2300 (11:00pm)". That is so true!

Once you arrive at MOS school you'll be assigned billeting (a room to stay in). When transferring to a school or a new duty station you do have some control over when you arrive. Before you leave your previous duty station you'll work with administrators to schedule your travel. I highly recommend you arrange your travel so that you arrive to your school one or two days before the course starts. This will give you time to get settled in your room (quarters) and also give you time to walk around, get to know the place a little and find the location of your class. I did this for every course I attended throughout my career, regardless of my rank, and it made the change in my location and daily routine much easier.

The formal school environment is much like boot camp. Instructors keep a tight leash on students during the day. In the evenings you'll usually have considerable freedom to do what you like. Any violations of conduct, whether on or off duty, are almost always dealt with severely at a formal school. If you're going to screw up or make a mistake, a formal school is not the place to do it.

Going to a formal school is just like going to college or high school except you are functioning in a very rigid social structure the entire time. I've found that the best way to be successful in a formal school is to adopt the following outlooks:

- Maintain your military bearing. Speak formally and be respectful to everyone.

- Maintain your military appearance. Make sure your uniforms are pressed, keep your hair cut and look like you're supposed to look.

- Work hard. Put forth maximum effort to learn what you're there to learn.

- If you're learning the material without much difficulty, help someone that is having a hard time (There will always be *someone* having a hard time).

- Do not fornicate (have sex with) with fellow students or instructors. This can only lead to problems regardless of your gender.

- Use your free time to exercise, rest or see the sites of the local area.

All formal schools are similar in that your main focus at these schools is to learn the subject material. Where Boot Camp and MCT are basic training to be a Marine, your formal school is your basic training to do the job that the Marine Corps needs you to do. Therefore, this school is very important for your professional competence. So act like it and do your best to learn everything you can.

Each MOS school has a different length. Some schools are 4 weeks long. Some schools are 63 weeks long. A few examples are: Field Radio Operator School in 29 Palms, CA is/was 10 weeks long. Chinese Language school at the Defense Language Institute (DLI) in Monterey, CA is/was 63 weeks long.

Some MOS's have several formal schools. If you're going to be a Cryptographic Technician, you might go to a basic electronics course (6 months), then a radio technician course (4 months), then a Crypto Technician course (8 months), totaling 1.5 years of training after Boot Camp and before you make it to your first Fleet Marine Force (FMF) unit.

Some jobs require multiple schools in different locations. If you're an infantry Marine and you get accepted to the

Reconnaissance field, you may find yourself going to Army Jump School at Fort Bragg, NC, then Pathfinder School in Fort Knox, KY, then scuba school in San Diego. Of course, this doesn't happen right away. Recon only takes seasoned Marines that have already been to their first duty station.

Some MOS's have a formal school then a period of on-the-job-training (OJT). Air Traffic Control (ATC) is a good example of this. ATC School is about 4 months long in Pensacola, FL. After that you go to your duty station and start training. Depending on the ATC facility you go to, it could take you 1 to 1.5 years to get qualified in the Control Tower and up to 2 years to get trained through the Radar Facility. It could take you 3.5 years to become fully qualified through an ATC facility after boot camp. Well, if Boot Camp and MCT are 4 months long, you might get fully qualified as a Controller about 2 months before you get out of the Marine Corps if you signed up on a 4 year contract… **and that's IF you didn't go on any deployments**. That's why Air Traffic Control usually requires a first enlistment of 6 years.

Formal schools are designed to successfully teach Marines a specific skill. The teaching methods are such that they should be able to teach a Marine the required skills even if he/she meets only the minimum standards of entry into the field. If someone's ASVAB score is on the low side and they are just barely eligible to go into a specific field, that school's curriculum is design to be teachable to the lowest or least qualified Marine. Don't worry about the difficulty of these schools. If you qualify to go to them, you'll be able to pass them with a little effort. As if to get this point across, most school instructors start off the class by saying something like, "This is one of the most technical/difficult/complicated schools in the Marine Corps. You're here because you're some of the smartest/most qualified Marines in the Corps".

Bottom line: Don't screw up, but don't sweat the school. Just show up ready to go and do your best.

## 5 HITTING THE FLEET

First thing to remember when you're about to hit the fleet is, don't be a dumb-ass. Often, when a Marine gets out of school, they show up at the first duty station thinking they can go hog wild because no one is micro-managing their day. These are usually the famous last thoughts of those that make an error in judgment early in their career.

Once you hit the fleet, everything you do is 100% your responsibility. Yes, you will have NCO's that will often try to handle any indiscretions "on the lowest level", but if you truly screw up, there's nothing any NCO is going to be able to do to fix it for you. So, don't screw up.

Once you get passed your physical and cultural assimilation into the Marine Corps, you'll find that the Marine Corps is actually a pretty easy job. You'll never have any doubt about **where** you're supposed to be or **when** you're supposed to be there. You're duties will usually be the same day to day, yet every day will usually be a little different.

So, upon arrival at your first duty station, objective number one is to get administratively processed into the unit. Every unit will usually hand you a "check-in" sheet which lists every office and location that you must check in to. The check-in process should not take more than 2 or 3 days, but often you'll find yourself at the mercy of billet-holders that are not on-hand when you go to check-in with them. Don't worry. Just get what you can done and try again the next day. There will usually be more than one person that can check you in, so ask around if the primary person isn't available.

Once you're checked, you'll start working. For the new fleet Marine, this will be the first time you start to actually do your job after learning the basics of that job at your MOS school. You should know that, although you just graduated MOS school, you probably still know little to nothing about the actual job you will be doing, so act accordingly. Start from day one learning the ropes. Your peers and NCO's should be able to give you direct guidance on the tasks required to be successful in your work section, whatever your job may be.

If you're checking in to a new unit, but it's not your first duty station, it's best to be humble, reserved and keep your mouth shut until you've had time to look around and get a handle on how things are done in your new unit. Once you get the lay of the land and a firm handle on the unit's mission, by all means take action to make adjustments as needed within your positions' realm of authority. In other words, if you're a Cpl, don't go up to the GySgt on day 3 and ask him why he wasn't at work at 0730. I've been there and made that mistake… when I was a Cpl I had gigantic balls, but you don't want the kind of specialized attention you'll get by doing something stupid like that, trust me.

The bottom line is, once you hit your first duty station, the buck stops with you. If you fail to do what you're supposed to do and be where you're supposed to be, it's your responsibility and your fault that you failed to perform.

In fact, that brings me to one of the MOST IMPROTANT pieces of advice I can give to any Marine, regardless of rank. This information must have been Top Secret at some point, because I swear that most people these days act like they've never heard of it before, the concept seems so foreign to them. **The Secret is this**: If you get caught screwing up, failing, not performing or not being where you are supposed to be (or caught doing ANYTHING wrong), there is only one answer you should give to the person confronting you. **That answer is simply, "It's 100% my fault".** Then apologize and take whatever action you need to take to make sure that it never happens again.

Read those last two sentences again. I can't over-state how important this is. I've learned this from experience. People can't continue to yell at you if you just come out and admit that you screwed up. Take responsibility for it and own it! It's those that deny fault, blame others and point fingers that end up getting hammered far harder than those that just accept the mistake and try to move on.

Shit happens to everyone. Everyone makes mistakes. The character of a Marine can be seen clearly in the way they handle the mistakes they make. So, the question you have to ask yourself is, how do you want your peers, supervisors and juniors to see you? Will they view you as an irresponsible jerk that blames everyone and everything else for their mistakes, or will they see you as a go-to Marine that does his/her best to get the job done, even in the face of difficulty?

How they view you is completely up to you. What choice will you make?

After you've gotten the hang of your unit and your daily routine, it's important to focus on self improvement. There's a reason that "Know yourself and seek self improvement" is the first leadership principal on the list. It's really important for your welfare, the welfare of your Marines, and your future in the Marine Corps that you understand your limitations and take action to try and improve.

Luckily for us, the Marine Corps offers many opportunities for self improvement, both at your own pace and with formal training courses. In fact, the Marine Corps actually mandates a minimum amount of additional training for Marines as they progress though their careers.

While the Marines Corps requirements for additional leadership training continue to evolve, there are many ways to improve yourself in the eyes of the Marine Corps. Here's a small list of things you could do off the top of my head, but there are also many other options:

1. Get a college degree (Tuition Assistance, Graduate Degree Programs, etc.)

2. MCI's: Marine Corps Institute correspondence courses.

3. Advanced MOS schools (not all MOS's have them, but most do).

4. Go to the leadership course appropriate for your grade (Not optional as I write this).

5. Improve your PFT/CFT scores. (Totally, 100% within YOUR control.)

6. Improve your rifle/pistol score.

7. Improve your MCMAP certification.

8. Improve your Swim Qualification designation.

In my opinion, as a Marine, the most important things to be good at are: 1) Leadership, 2) Physical Fitness, and 3) Marksmanship. However, none of that stuff is worth anything if you don't have the knowledge to apply those skills. Also, the MOS of a Marine also requires a certain level of technical proficiency and competence, so don't overlook the skills required to be good at your MOS, otherwise you may find yourself great at the "Marine Stuff", but lacking severely in your ability to accomplish your mission, which is NOT GOOD considering Marines are known for their ability to accomplish the mission! Note: Any Marine can fall into this trap, but in my experience this most often happens to Marines that leave their primary MOS for a few years either on a temporary assignment or a "B" billet, like Recruiting, Marine Security Guard or Drill Instructor duty.

Being a Marine is like having two full time jobs. On one hand you're expected to be a very fit, hard-core, intelligent, steely-eyed, unstoppable killing machine… on the other hand you're expected to be a highly professional, technically proficient (fill in your MOS here). So, you really have to look at it as though you have two professions, unless you are infantry. The Marines Corps trains as if "Every Marine is a Rifleman". So, if your primary job isn't a Rifleman, you've got some more work to do, either becoming more proficient as a Rifleman, or becoming more proficient in your MOS skills, or both.

This may start to sound like not such a fun job, when you think about all that is expected of you as a Marine, but this is the reality.

Next, you'll want to take advantage of any opportunity that comes up. And I mean **any** opportunity. You can get the hang of jumping on opportunities almost any time, all you have to do is step forward and volunteer any time someone asks for volunteers. Now, there is an old theory, seen by those that have even a little military experience, that you **never** volunteer for anything. I agree that this is the way to be if your primary goal is to avoid shitty jobs. However, if your goal is to get the most experience possible in the shortest amount of time, you should volunteer for everything that comes up.

Yes, you'll have your share of shitty jobs, but you'll also have your share of irreplaceable experiences. For example, I was in Okinawa in 2005 and had a deployment come up. We asked for volunteers. All we told our Marines was that it was a deployment. Two Marines stepped forward as volunteers. It turned out that these two Marines got to deploy immediately to Pakistan.

This opportunity came up because, on 8 October in 2005, a magnitude 7.6 earthquake hit the Kashmir region of Pakistan, creating an enormous humanitarian crisis. Our Marines, both Air

Traffic Controllers, were attached to a special MAGTF and provided LZ control support to Marine Helicopters providing humanitarian aid.

At the time, we had wars going in Iraq and Afghanistan, but very few Marines (if any) ever ventured into Pakistan. Because these two Marines volunteered, they got to experiences a deployment that the other 450 active duty Marine Air Traffic Controllers never would.

So, the moral of the story is, if you volunteer, you'll have both good and bad experiences. You'll also find that the good experiences tend to really out-weigh the bad ones. If you want to skate through your Marines Corps career with as little difficulty as possible, don't volunteer and do only what you have to. If you want to get the most out of your experience, volunteer for everything! If you volunteer, those that chose not to will be laughing at you when you end up scrubbing toilets, but when you get back from Thailand or Korea and share your stories with them, they'll wish they had volunteered, I guarantee it.

There are all sorts of opportunities that come up. Try to put forth a maximum effort every day, and your supervisors will tend to think of you when they come up. One of the easiest opportunities that you can take advantage of are advanced training courses. These are usually completely dependent on which MOS you have, but most MOS's have some sort of advanced schools. For example: if you're an Infantryman, advanced schools that will eventually become available to you might include Squad Leader School, Platoon Sergeants Course, Helicopter Rope Suspension Training (HRST) Master Course, Cold Weather Training, Jungle Environment Survival Training (JEST) Course, Mountain Warfare Training, Sniper School, Recon Marine Course, Jump School, Dive School, Pathfinder School and many more.

Every MOS has advanced schools like this, but most of them have to do with your primary MOS. I've never met a Marine in any MOS that wouldn't LOVE to go to any of the infantry schools I mentioned above, but there are MOS's that may never have the opportunity to go to any of those specific courses, so hopefully you'll choose your MOS carefully.

Over the years that I was an active duty Marine, things really changed. We went from having no personal computers in 1990, to having them on almost every desk by 2000. Along with the increased productivity potential of the desktop computer, came an increase in the expected level of work from work sections, AND an increase in training requirements for the individual Marine. So, compared to the early 1990's and before then, most mid-level managers, SNCO's and Officers are up to their eye-balls in administrative paperwork, most of the time, more-so now than any time in the past.

Also, the training requirements required for each Marine have increased tremendously during the same time period. We use to worry about Rifle Range, Swim Qual, Gas Chamber, PFT and BST each year for every Marine. When I retired in 2010, we had all the same stuff, plus extended NBC classes, weekly MCMAP classes, Equal Opportunity training, Anti-Terrorism Training, Training and Readiness events requiring hundreds and even thousands of hours of study, preparation and execution tied to your primary MOS, and much, much more.

If all that weren't enough, most Officers and Staff NCO's often find themselves serving in multiple billets, doing two or more jobs simultaneously, making it VERY difficult for them to spend quality time training with the NCO's and below. I've met many SNCO's and Officers that are "task saturated" to the point that they will never get caught up on all the tasks for all their jobs, even if they were to work

24 hours a day, 7 days a week for the rest of their careers. Many of them become burnt out and exhausted after years of trying to tread water.

So, if you choose to stay in and become a Staff NCO or an Officer, you should know that you will be expected to do far more every day than you were as an NCO. Be ready for it, and once you get use to it, try to make time to spend with your Marines during training. Spending time with the troops is far more valuable to you than doing a paper drill for some staff billet… just my opinion.

# 6 OPPORTUNITIES

Now that you've heard plenty about what not to do, let's talk about what you can do to make anything possible for you in the Marine Corps. It doesn't matter where you come from, how much money your family has or doesn't have, what your race, color, creed, religion, gender or sexual orientation is. The Marine Corps provides lots of opportunity for any Marine that is willing to reach out and seize it.

First, let's talk about promotion opportunities. I've got great news for you about promotions. Unlike some other services, as of 2012 promotions to PFC through Cpl (E-2 through E-4) are pretty much automatic, as long as you show up when and where you're suppose to and do what you're supposed to do. The Navy, for example requires testing of knowledge based material for promotions to almost all enlisted ranks. That's probably the only thing about the enlisted Navy other than SEAL training that is more stringent than in the Marines, so enjoy that little fact. Of course, you have to score well on all your annual training events to be eligible for promotion, so that may even things out considerably.

To be eligible for promotion, you must have a certain amount of months at your current rank (this is different for each rank and is listed in the Promotion Manual and the Basic Skill Training book, or BST) and not have anything in your record preventing you from being promoted. Things that can be placed in your record and prevent you from being promoted include: Non-Judicial Punishment (NJP), a Courts Martial, a civilian conviction of a crime, failure to pass one of the previously mentioned annual training events and tests, failing to meet the height and weight standards set by the Marine Corps, or a non-recommendation (Non-Rec) from your supervisors with some sort of documentation showing you are not ready for more responsibility. An unfavorable fitness report (Fit Rep) can also stop your promotion, but only Sergeants and above receive Fit Rep's.

Later promotions to Cpl and Sergeant are determined by a "cutting score". The cutting score is based on the scores you achieve on all your annual training events, your time in service and time in your current grade (or rank), AND the proficiency and conduct marks (Pro/Con marks) you are given semi-annually by your supervisors. A limited number of Marine Corps Institute Correspondence courses and College classes also count toward your cutting score. So, your performance on your PFT, CFT, Rifle Range, Swim Qual, MCMAP Belt, your Pro/Con marks, your seniority in rank and on active duty, and even how many MCI's you have completed will have a direct effect on your cutting score.

Each enlisted MOS within the Marine Corps has a specific structure and population level that the Marine Corps tries to maintain. For example, if you're a supply specialist, the Marine Corps already knows how many supply specialists they need to accomplish their mission. They know how many E-1 (Private) supply specialists they need. They know how many E-2 (Private 1st Class) supply specialists they need. They know how many E-3 (Lance Corporal) supply specialists they need and so on up through the highest rank of supply specialist that the Marine Corps employs. So, it would be accurate to say that the Corps knows not only how many supply specialists it needs in general, but also how many supply specialists it needs at each rank.

Each quarter (this time frame could be adjusted to monthly, yearly, semi-annually, or whatever, based on the needs of the Marine Corps), the Marines in charge of Manpower determine how many E-4 (Corporal) supply specialists they need to promote to Sergeant. Once that determination has been made, they take a list of all the supply specialists Corporals in the Marine Corps **that are eligible for promotion**, listed from the highest cutting score to the lowest (senior Corporals tend to have higher cutting scores, but seniority does not guarantee a high cutting score), then count backward down the list the number corporals they need to promote. The cutting score of the Marine they stop on becomes the cutting score "cut off" for the Corporals that will be promoted to Sergeant during that period.

For example, Manpower determines that they need to promote 50 supply specialists from Corporal to Sergeant next quarter. So they print off the list of Corporals in the supply specialist field, listed from senior Corporal to junior Corporal. They will usually filter this list to include only Corporals that are eligible for promotion. They count down from the top of the list down until they get to the 50th Marine

on the list. The cutting score of that 50th Marine becomes the cutting

score "cut off" for the supply specialist MOS for that next quarter.

That Marine, and every Corporal on the list with a higher cutting

score that is eligible for promotion will be promoted, unless

something happens between the date the cutting score comes out and

promotion day that makes a Marine in-eligible for promotion, like

failing an annual training event or getting a non-rec from your

Officer in Charge.

1 January, 1 April, 1 July or 1 October mark the beginning of

each fiscal quarter, and the last time I checked, these NCO

promotions occurred on these dates. Non-NCO promotions occur

monthly based on seniority and eligibility, and monthly for all ranks

from Staff Sergeant through Colonel based on a selection process.

But, like I mentioned before, these promotion dates could be

changed to monthly semi-annually or annually, based on the needs of

the Marine Corps, so check the promotion manual.

Ok, enough about regular promotions. I know those last few

pages might sound confusing to the fresh young mind that hasn't been exposed to the Corps for very long. Just read it again a few times and you'll get it. Also, I encourage you to look promotions up in both the promotion manual and the BST.

The last thing I'll tell you about regarding promotions is my explanation of Meritorious Promotions. I remember my recruiter mentioned Meritorious Promotions to me before I entered the Marine Corps and I thought he was crazy, because just the word "meritorious" sounded ridiculous and made up to me.

A meritorious promotion is a promotion that is awarded to a deserving Marine based on his or her merit or performance, usually before they become eligible for a normal promotion. The fact is, meritorious promotions can be had, relatively easily as an enlisted Marine. They are available to any enlisted rank, from Private to Staff Sergeant, and the only real requirement is that the Marine deserves to be promoted based on their performance.

I've seen generals meritoriously promote young Marines on the spot, after talking with them in the chow hall or in passing in other locations. Usually, meritorious promotions are delegated down, from Headquarters Marine Corps (HQMC) through the Generals and Colonels to the Battalion/Squadron or Company level. Then the

Battalion/Squadron or Company level Commander usually delegates

it further to their senior enlisted, typically a Sergeant Major (SgtMaj)

or First Sergeant (1st Sgt). That senior enlisted Marine will usually

hold some sort of "Board" in which they review the records of high

performing Marines within the unit to determine which one should

be promoted early.

At that level, there is usually only one meritorious promotion to

give away at each rank from PFC through Sgt, and I think NCO only

become available about once a quarter. So, if you want to be

promoted early, become a high performer. Meritorious promotions

to SSgt and GySgt usually only come along once a year and are only

awarded at the Division or Wing level or higher. This means that

each year, there are only 4 to 6 of these spot available throughout the

entire Marine Corps. As you can imagine, competition is very stiff for

SSgt and GySgt, so you really have to be a rock star Sgt or SSgt to

have a chance at either of them.

Last thing I'll mention about meritorious promotions is, as of

the date I published this book, there is also something called a

Meritorious Commissioning Program, or MCP. This is a program

that allows enlisted Marines to become officers, usually going direct to OCS upon acceptance into the program. You can find out more about current requirements for this and other officer programs from either your Career Retention Specialist (CRS) or from the appropriate Marine corps Publication. I recommend going straight to the publications, because all the officer programs have a ton of requirements that must be met in order to submit your package for consideration. It's best to look those requirements up yourself to ensure you're getting the full set of instructions.

Now, let's talk about opportunity within your specific MOS. Each MOS has very specific training requirements. Many MOS's these days have become extremely technical due to the extremely fast evolution of technology since the 1980's or so. Years and years ago, it use to be that the Marine Corps wanted Marines be extremely physically fit and to show up and do what their Officers told them to do. Today, Marine Corps jobs are more technical and specialized than ever.

Now, Marines are smarter and more technically trained than at any time in history. We have smart bombs, fire and forget missiles, computers, multi-million dollar weapons systems, artillery that can fire 20 miles over the horizon, counter artillery that can blast an enemy just seconds after they shoot at us, tanks that are driven by jet engines and computers, etc. The new world and the technology we use in it are complicated. That's why now, the Marine Corps wants Marines that can learn quickly, adapt and think for themselves using good judgment.

This new age of technology has made it necessary for Marine MOS's to be on the cutting edge of current and future technology. Therefore, most MOS's today have an initial school, followed by multiple, more advanced schools as Marines become more seasoned and experienced in their trade. These more advance schools are usually reserved for really smart or high performing first term Marines or Marines on the second and third enlistments.

Obviously, the additional training requirements for each MOS will be different based on the mission requirements laid out by the Commandant. At the moment, I can't think of a single MOS that I've come across in the last 20 years that doesn't have some sort of advanced school. So, regardless of your MOS, the odds are that your boss will, at some point, be asked to submit a Marine for an advanced school seat. Who do you think they'll pick? Well, if you're a high performer, and a go-to Marine, you will at the very least be at the top of their list. Unfortunately, leaders often have to weigh who they send to these schools against their operational commitments. So, you may find yourself choosing between a deployment and a school. Most of the time, the choice won't be yours, but try to understand if you're a top performer and get chosen for a deployment instead of a school. Marine leaders NEED those go-to Marines! There aren't always a lot of them, and if you're one, you are an asset. So the best thing to do is let your leaders know YOU WANT TO GO to whatever advanced school your MOS needs, if that's what you want to do.

Opportunities in the form of other duty usually show up around your second or third enlistment. The most common of them are called "B" Billets. Duties that fall into this category are Drill Instructor Duty, Recruiting Duty and Marine Security Guard (MSG) Duty. Once you've been to Boot Camp, there's no question what you would be doing as a Drill Instructor.

Recruiting Duty is something every Marine should have at least seen done, although I hear that it's a lot less pleasant than the other two due to the constant pressure of recruitment quotas.

I've heard MSG described as the "best kept secret in the Marine Corps". MSG Marines provide security to the United States Department of State at Embassies around the world. It's supposed to be some amazing duty, if you can get it. There is also an added amount of danger. During a three year MSG tour, you'll serve for 1.5 years at a "hardship duty station" (a place that sucks, or where many of the locals or local government might be hostile toward the United States), and 1.5 years at a friendlier location (think Europe, New Zealand, and Japan).

Given the choice, I'd rather go MSG than anything else. In fact, I was selected for it when I was a GySgt, but my monitor thought a trip to Iraq would be better for me.

There are other, lesser known duties that come up. Some that I've seen in the last few years include, MCT Troop Handler, School of Infantry Instructor, SNCO Academy Instructor, OCS/TBS Instructor, the occasional secret squirrel duty and Foreign Country

Trainer/Liaison duty. All these usually look for a very specific type of Marine, and they don't come up that often, but they are out there.

.

Educational opportunities are also available. First of all, once you get established in the Fleet and you're doing your job, you could attend college classes. The Marine Corps provides tuition assistance to active duty Marines. Most recently they've been paying 100% tuition for Marines while they're on active duty. If you're able to take college classes, do it. Life when you get out will be a hell of a lot easier if you have a degree, or even if you're close to having one.

You can also get out after your first enlistment, go to college on your GI Bill, then re-enter the Marines as an Officer. I have a number of friends I was enlisted with that got out, went to college and are now flying jets and helicopters for the Corps.

The Marine Corps also has a few Officer programs designed to give enlisted Marines a leg up, an into the Officer ranks. Marine Corps Order (MCO) 1040.43 spells out the application requirements for both the Enlisted Commissioning Program (ECP) and the Meritorious Commissioning Program (MCP). There is also the Broadened Opportunity for Officer Selection and Training (BOOST)

Program. Last one I know of is the Marine Corps Enlisted Commissioning Education Program (MECEP). The appropriate Marine Corps Orders can be referenced for details on any of these programs, and I strongly urge you to look them up and read them for yourself.

Another, more informal education is something you'll gain just by spending time on active duty. **Pay attention to this**, it'll save you years of experience from the school of hard knocks: **If you ever, ever have a question about a Marine Corps program, policy or regulation, look up MCO 5000.14, Marine Corps Administrative Procedures**. The short title is MCAP. This single publication lists all publications currently used by the Marine Corps. You can find a reference for any subject you need to look up within this Manual. Use it! Do not rely of your Admin guys, or a CRS to tell you what the current policies are. If you can read, you can look them up. When you do so, you're learning about whatever policy you're concerned with, directly from the Commandant of the Marine Corps! If you trust others to interpret regulations for you, you subject yourself to their interpretation. What if the person you're asking is wrong?

Worse, what if the person you're asking was told by someone else, and now he's telling you?

The bottom line on the MCAP manual is, you don't want to trust your career and your success to some guy that may or may not know what he's talking about, do you? Don't mistake this for a respect thing either. If a GySgt from admin tells you that you "don't rate" BAH (or whatever), respectfully thank him for the info and leave. Then, at home or off duty, look up the appropriate order and read it. The order will tell you who rates what, and that's the policy for all Marines. If you do find out that a senior Marine gave you bad information and you have to go back to them to get something done, be tactful! The last thing you want to do is piss off the guy you need to submit a request for you.

Last thing about written orders… There are also locally written orders, like Base Orders (BO), Air Station Orders (ASO), Division Orders (DO), Wing Orders (WO), Battalion Orders (BO) and so on. Any Officer with a command has the authority to write a written order. Just make sure that you read the pertinent local orders on the subject, as well as the Marine Corps Orders. Local orders can be

MORE RESTRICTIVE than Marine Corps Orders, but not less restrictive, unless the local commander has special permission.

## 7 GETTING PROMOTED

Everybody, regardless of the reason they joined the Corps, wants to be promoted. I even know some E-9's that would love to see the Marine Corps institute an E-10 rank.

So, the question is, how do you go about getting promoted? I've already answered a bit of that in previous chapters, but here's a little more to chew on...

As previously mentioned, all you have to do to get promoted prior to reaching the NCO ranks is show up when you're supposed to show up and do what you're supposed to do. It really is that simple. Yes, you can get promoted faster by being a high level performer. Score high on all your training events, be the go-to Marine and sooner or later your bosses are going to notice that you are meritorious promotion material.

Once you become a Cpl things change a bit. For one thing, you're now a Non-Commissioned Officer and have considerably more responsibility when it comes to leadership. So, what makes you a better leader the day after you pick up Cpl than you were the day before you picked up Cpl? The answer is, not a damn thing. You are no better than you were before, people just treat you differently because you have a different title. The trick is to try to live up to that title.

In many locations Marine senior enlisted leaders have put training programs in place to try to ensure that new Cpl's are equipped to handle the job. This Cpl's course should be attended by new Cpl's as soon as possible after promotion. Some places also have a LCpl's Course. If you have the opportunity to attend them, do so.

If you're not in a location that has a Cpl's (or LCpl's) Course available, there are other methods of figuring out how to behave in your new roll. First, your SNCO should be speaking to you about this the day you get promoted, so he/she should be able to give you some specific recommendations based on the specific personalities you work with. Next, if you've been promoted to Cpl, you've surly been in the Marines for at least a year or two, right? Think about all the best Cpl's you've worked with and the things they did that made you think they were good. Then, think about all the worst Cpl's you've worked with and the things they did that made them bad. Then incorporate the good things into your "tool bag" and remove the bad things from your "tool bag". Lastly, use these tools for two things: 1) To accomplish your mission, and 2) To ensure the welfare of your Marines. Notice I didn't say "to hook up your friends", or "harass Marines you don't like". That shit just isn't right.

Once you become a NCO, ALL your relationships must change. You'll have friends that are still Lance Corporals, but you, and they, need to know up front that the relationship has been changed and that it's simply not a matter of choice for either of you. If you try to hold on to the friendship and expect it to be the same, you are in for a rude awakening.

The Marine Corps has a policy of not fraternizing with junior ranks in general, but they really frown upon NCO's hanging out with Non-NCO's, SNCO's hanging out with NCO's or Non-NCO's, and they're EXTREMELY anal about Officers hanging out with enlisted Marines. Don't misunderstand this. All Marines share a professional bound. We are all willing to lay down our lives to protect our nation and our fellow Marines. We are all brothers and sisters in arms, but that professionalism can only be maintained if we keep a strictly professional working relationship designed to accomplish the mission and look after the welfare of the troops.

If you try to force the maintenance for an informal, buddy-buddy relationship with a junior Marine, sooner or later it's going to blow up in your face. It always happens, it doesn't matter how smart you think you are (the smart ones always think they are the exception). The fact is that human nature dictates behavior. When a person of authority is less personally familiar, we are more apt to accept their authority without question. When a person of authority is familiar, we tend to be more willing to question them. When a person of authority is a friend, we will question them for sure, it's just a matter of when.

So, the Marine Corps solution for this problem of human nature is an appropriate one. Don't fraternize with Marines outside of your rank window (Non-NCO, NCO, Staff NCO, Officer). It just never works, no matter how mature people think they are. I could write a whole book filled with examples that I witnessed, proving this... Just take my word for it and don't do it.

Last note on fraternization pertains to intimate relationships. I didn't say "male/female" relationships because lawmakers have given gay men and women permission to serve openly in the military. Everything I said above applies to anyone engaging in a personal/intimate relationship. Most commands will outright forbid intimate relationship amongst Marines of different ranks, and even frown upon relationships between those of same or similar ranks (like Cpl/Sgt or PFC/LCpl). The one way around this is, you can generally date a person of a similar rank as long as they are in a different USMC unit, or different service all together. You are still restricted to enlisted (if you're enlisted) or officers (if you're an officer), but dating someone in another unit generally removes the potential for conflict of interest, and has been deemed 'not forbidden' by the Marine Corps regulations, last time I checked. You might want to check yourself. It's been a while since I looked that one up.

I'll talk more about intimate relationships later, but for now, I recommend avoiding them if you can, and if you can't, be very careful who you choose the engage with.

Back to things you *should* do… as a Cpl (actually, as *any* rank) you should be looking forward to the next rank and working towards that promotion. The best thing you can do as a Cpl to immediately make yourself more qualified for that promotion is get to the Cpl's Course immediately (if not sooner!) and do the MCI's that are required for BOTH the rank of Cpl and the rank of Sgt. Yes, I said do them both. When I'm considering a Cpl for promotion to Sgt, or for a meritorious Sgt board, the Marine that's preparing ahead of time will always look better right from the start.

Here's a road map to picking up your next rank. It applies to any rank, generally, but in this case, I'll be using the rank of Cpl as the example.

Plan of Action for Cpl Just-promoted:

**Day 1**: You get promoted. After the ceremony, go speak with your SNCO, find out when the next Cpl's course is going, and find out what you have to do to make sure you have a seat in it. Next, order all the MCI's required to be promoted to Sgt (if you haven't already completed them. If you have, order the MCI's required for promotion to SSgt).

**Day 2**: Sit down and evaluate yourself. Ask a SNCO for a Pro/Con worksheet and fill it out on yourself. Honestly rate yourself pointing out both areas you're doing well in, and areas you need improvement in. Rate yourself as a Marine, not as a LCpl or Cpl.

**Day 3**: Review the Pro/Con marks you gave yourself. Make a list of things you can do to improve the areas that need improvement. (Hint: If you are not getting a maximum score on something, you could improve.) Look for ways to improve your PFT, CFT, Swim Qual, Rifle and/or Pistol qual, BST, Primary MOS skills and anything else you can think of. Pull out a calendar and write down those things you could do to improve, and use that as a schedule to execute that improvement. Take immediate action on this schedule thing. Don't procrastinate! This should occupy your off time for at least the next 90 days.

**Day 90**: You should be well on your way to improving yourself, based on your self improvement schedule. By now, you should also be graduating Cpl's course, or at least attending the course. Now is not the time to let up. Seek out you SNCOIC or OIC and ask for a counseling session. Take your self-improvement schedule with you to the counseling session. Explain to your senior(s) what you've come up with, what you've completed, then ask them for input. Find out what they think you could do to become a better Marine. If they give you something actionable like "do more MCI's" or "improve your run time" then add that to your schedule and start working towards improvement. If they give you something related to behavior like "take the initiative more often", then take that to heart and do your best to make that happen every day.

**Day 180**: By now you should have had at least one counseling session, and most likely one evaluation period (Pro/Con marks, or a FITREP). Compare those marks to your previous evaluation. Now, compare any improvement or decline to your self-improvement schedule, and see what you can adjust, include or replace to make your schedule more effective.

If you've done the things I've outlined above and had success at improving yourself, your leaders may start to consider you for a meritorious promotion. They may not, but they may. The steps above outline a path to success, but your attitude and behavior will also play a big part in what opportunities will come your way. If participation in a meritorious board is offered to you, take it!

Don't be a douche like I was when I was a Cpl and say "no, I'm too busy with work to do a meritorious board". I picked up Cpl meritoriously, did a lateral move to another MOS and when I was recommended for meritorious Sgt boards I said no. What happened was, they sent another Cpl from my shop to the board and he won. Unfortunately he was a total dumbass. So, because I 1) wanted to be lazy and 2) didn't feel like I deserved a meritorious promotion as someone that had little time in a new MOS, someone ELSE (who was less qualified than I) got the promotion. Moral of the story: If you choose to be a lazy douche, you will soon be led by a dumbass, instead of leading yourself.

By the way, meritorious promotions are NOT based on your MOS; regular promotions are. So don't ever think that because you don't know everything there is to know about your MOS that you aren't meritorious promotion material. You are as much as anyone else is!

If you do ever end up on a meritorious promotion board, you better do your fucking homework. Don't be the Marine that goes into the board and gets every question you're asked wrong. Meritorious boards are hard work. You've got to make sure your uniform looks PERFECT. Your behavior inside the board must be nearly perfect, and you better know the questions they ask you.

These boards aren't that hard if you're prepared. Each member of the board asks you several general knowledge questions. You'll almost never be asked anything outside of what someone of the promotion rank should know anyway, but if you've read through a BST lately you've probably noticed that there's a lot of shit in there! Back when I was a LCpl studying for this, the BST was only one book that applied to all Marines. It was about 4 inches thick and was absolutely packed with information. It took me several weeks to memorize that book, but memorize it I did! So, I recommend you do the same.

Last thing about meritorious boards: as a SSgt, GySgt and a MSgt, I've sat on and run many, many meritorious boards. Over the several years I spent doing this I noticed one thing; most Marines that stepped in front of our boards missed at least 70% of the questions they were asked. For god's sake, if you are selected to compete on a promotion board, do your homework. Know the BST and the mission of your unit inside and out, backwards and sideways. If you do, I guarantee you'll be noticed.

The best piece of advice I was ever given regarding how to get promoted fast was, "take on the responsibility of the next rank", meaning that I should act as the next higher rank should act. That doesn't mean you run around acting like a Gunny when you're a LCpl. That means if you're a Cpl, know the things that a Sergeant should know and act as a good Sergeant should act.

# 8 LEADERSHIP

Taught from the second week of boot camp, leadership is THE MOST crucial skill you will learn in the Marines. Leadership is an attribute that is so important in the military environment, that the Marine Corps will make efforts to continue to develop your leadership skill for the entire time you're an active Marine. This should tell you something. Leadership, specifically GOOD leadership, is extremely important to success and survival of both you as an individual, and the Marine Corps.

I've read numerous books on the subject of leadership that have said leadership is a natural born skill that some people possess, and some people don't. In my opinion, that is complete bullshit. If that were true, the Marine Corps would spend time trying to recruit natural born leaders. The truth is, leaders are made, not born. Yes, there are people that naturally learn faster than others. Some take to leadership faster, some to languages, and some people learn physical movements faster. But the bottom line is, everyone learns. The Marine Corps wants to teach people to become Marines and then teach Marines how to lead.

After 20 years of service to the Corps, I can say with confidence that the Marine Corps Institution does a reasonably good job teaching leadership to Marines. That being said, I've also noticed some people will spend a whole career trying to learn the art of leadership and still not understand it. In fact, it took me 16 years and a trip to a combat zone under the command of a horrible leader to REALLY get it. Everyone learns at different rates and from different experiences. For some, leadership clicks in their mind early, for others it could take a lifetime.

The Marine Corps is continuously evolving. One thing it usually does pretty well is learning from its mistakes. Usually termed "Lessons Learned", this process of debriefing operational staff members allows them to learn from things that went wrong and implement corrective action for future operations. During my career, leadership training has changed considerably. In 1990, leadership training was primarily done in basic training and "on-the-job". They did have "NCO School" in which Sergeants and senior Corporals received formal leadership training. They also had several correspondence courses through the "Marine Corps Institute" that focused on teaching various levels of combat leadership. Two that come to mind are the Warfighting series and the Command and Staff College series, both intended for senior Staff NCO's and junior Officers.

Today, leadership training in the Marine Corps is significantly more prevalent. As I write this, there is a leadership course for almost every rank you can be promoted to on the enlisted side, and officers are expected to earn a master's degree through one of the various advanced education courses if they intend to make the Corps a career.

Some of the leadership courses that exist as of 2012 are:

- Lance Corporals Course (very few installations have this).

- Corporals Course (Provided at the base level. Some locations don't have this).

- Sergeants Course.

- SNCO Career Course (for SSgt's).

- SNCO Advanced Course (for GySgt's).

- The E-8 Seminar (For MSgt's and 1stSgt's)

- Command & Staff College (For junior officers and senior enlisted, it's a correspondents course but it is usually proctored weekly by an experienced officer that has actually attended the resident Command & Staff Course or the Naval War College).

- Naval Post-Graduate School (NPS, Officers accepted to this school go to Monterey CA for 18 months of graduate work in a specific area of study).

- Naval War College (another Officer graduate program, heavy on warfare and international relations).

I've personally participated in all of these programs except for the last two, but hands down, the best leadership school/course I attended in my entire career was the course I attended to become an Equal Opportunity program manager in Okinawa, Japan. The EO Marines that worked for each General on the island came together and produced a course that I found absolutely life changing. I hope that one day the rest of the Marine Corps adopts that system of training EO Marines, but as far as I know, Okinawa from 2007 to 2010 was the only place and time that specific course style was offered. However, if you get the chance to be trained as an EO, take it! And no, you don't need to have some specific ethnic background to be an EO. I'm a white guy and I've been told I did a pretty good job.

As you can see, the Marine Corps has made an effort to better train both their officers and their enlisted Marines in leadership, some would say by necessity. The world is a different place today than it was in 1990 or 1970. We have computers, cell phones, unmanned aviation assets, non-lethal weapons and other high tech gadgets.

One thing about the Marines and our purpose will never change though, and that's the need for hardcore warriors that are willing and capable of bringing a lethal fight to the enemy. All these new gadgets, tactics and training requirements we've seen appear over the last few decades make the Marines more than a full time job. It really is a complete lifestyle. After you join, you'll find that there is so much going on each and every day, that it's an absolute necessity to keep Marines grounded in basic leadership.

So, what is leadership? I believe on a small scale, it's the art of persuading other people to do your bidding. On a larger scale, I believe it's the art of making people commit to an idea or goal that is

greater than themselves and encouraging them to act accordingly.

The Marine Corps has broken down "leadership" into a group of

traits and principles that they say every Marine leader should possess

and follow to be effective. Here's an excerpt from MCRP 6-11B

w/CH 1 describing the traits and principles of leadership, as the

Marine Corps sees them:

1. **14 LEADERSHIP TRAITS**

   The fourteen leadership traits can be remembered with the
   acronym **JJ-DIDTIEBUCKLE:**

   - <u>J</u>ustice
   - <u>J</u>udgment
   - <u>D</u>ependability
   - <u>I</u>nitiative
   - <u>D</u>ecisiveness
   - <u>T</u>act
   - <u>I</u>ntegrity
   - <u>E</u>nthusiasm
   - <u>B</u>earing
   - <u>U</u>nselfishness
   - <u>C</u>ourage
   - <u>K</u>nowledge
   - <u>L</u>oyalty
   - <u>E</u>ndurance

   **<u>J</u>ustice:**
   *Definition* - Giving reward and punishment according to the
   merits of the case in question. The ability to administer a
   system of rewards and punishments impartially and
   consistently.

*Significance* - The quality of displaying fairness and impartiality is critical in order to gain the trust and respect of subordinates and maintain discipline and unit cohesion, particularly in the exercise of responsibility.

*Example* - Fair apportionment of tasks by a squad leader during field day.

## Judgment:

*Definition* - The ability to weigh facts and possible courses of action in order to make sound decisions.

*Significance* - Sound judgment allows a leader to make appropriate decisions in the guidance and training of his/her Marines and the employment of his/her unit. A Marine who exercises good judgment weighs the positives and negatives of a decision accordingly when making appropriate decisions.

*Example* - A Marine properly apportions his/her liberty time in order to relax as well as to study.

## Dependability:

*Definition* - The certainty of proper performance of duty.

*Significance* - The quality that permits a senior to assign a task to a junior with the understanding that it will be accomplished with minimum supervision.

*Example* - The squad leader ensures that his/her squad falls out in the proper uniform without having been told to by the platoon sergeant.

## Initiative:

*Definition* - Taking action in the absence of orders.

*Significance* - Since an NCO often works without close supervision; emphasis is placed on being a self-starter. Initiative is a founding principle of Marine Corps Warfighting philosophy.

*Example* - In the unexplained absence of the platoon sergeant, an NCO takes charge of the platoon and carries out the training schedule.

## Decisiveness:

*Definition* - Ability to make decisions promptly and to announce them in a clear, forceful manner.

*Significance* - The quality of character which guides a person to accumulate all available facts in a circumstance, weigh the facts, and choose and announce an alternative which seems best. It is often better that a decision be made promptly than a potentially better one be made at the expense of more time. *Example* - A leader, who sees a potentially dangerous situation developing, immediately takes action to prevent injury from occurring.

## Tact:
*Definition* - The ability to deal with others in a manner that will maintain good relations and avoid offense. More simply stated, tact is the ability to say and do the right thing at the right time.
*Significance* - The quality of consistently treating peers, seniors, and subordinates with respect and courtesy is a sign of maturity. Tact allows commands, guidance, and opinions to be expressed in a constructive and beneficial manner. This deference must be extended under all conditions regardless of true feelings.
*Example* - A Marine discreetly points out a mistake in drill to an NCO by waiting until after the unit has been dismissed and privately asking which of the two methods are correct.

## Integrity:
*Definition* - Uprightness of character and soundness of moral principles. The quality of truthfulness and honesty.
*Significance* - A Marine's word is his/her bond. Nothing less than complete honesty in all of your dealings with subordinates, peers, and superiors is acceptable.
*Example* - A Marine who uses the correct technique on the obstacle course, even when he/she cannot be seen by the evaluator.

## Enthusiasm:
*Definition* - The display of sincere interest and exuberance in the performance of duty.
*Significance* - Displaying interest in a task and optimism that can be successfully completed greatly enhances the likelihood that the task will be successfully completed.
*Example* - A Marine who leads a chant or offers to help carry a load that is giving someone great difficulty while on a hike

despite being physically tired, he encourages his fellow Marines to persevere.

## Bearing:

*Definition* - Creating a favorable impression in carriage, appearance, and personal conduct at all times.

*Significance* - The ability to look, talk, and act like a leader whether or not these manifestations indicate one's true feelings.

*Example* - Wearing clean uniforms, boots, and collar devices. Avoiding profane and vulgar language. Keeping a trim, fit appearance.

## Unselfishness:

*Definition* - Avoidance of providing for one's own comfort and personal advancement at the expense of others.

*Significance* - The quality of looking out for the needs of your subordinates before your own is the essence of leadership. This quality is not to be confused with putting these matters ahead of the accomplishment of the mission.

*Example* - An NCO ensures all members of his unit have eaten before he does, or if water is scarce, he will share what he has and ensure that others do the same.

## Courage:

*Definition* - Courage is a mental quality that recognizes fear of danger or criticism, but enables a Marine to proceed in the face of danger with calmness and firmness.

*Significance* - Knowing and standing for what is right, even in the face of popular disfavor. The business of fighting and winning wars is a dangerous one; the importance of courage on the battlefield is obvious.

*Example* - Accepting criticism for making subordinates field day for an extra hour to get the job done correctly.

## Knowledge:

*Definition* - Understanding of a science or an art. The range of one's information, including professional knowledge and understanding of your Marines.

*Significance* - The gaining and retention of current developments in military and naval science and world affairs is important for your growth and development.

*Example* - The Marine who not only knows how to maintain and operate his assigned weapon, but also knows how to use the other weapons and equipment in the unit.

## Loyalty:

*Definition* - The quality of faithfulness to country, Corps, unit, seniors, subordinates and peers.

*Significance* - The motto of the Marine Corps is *Semper Fidelis*, Always Faithful. You owe unswerving loyalty up and down the chain of command.

*Example* - A Marine displaying enthusiasm in carrying out an order of a senior, though he may privately disagree with it.

## Endurance:

*Definition* - The mental and physical stamina measured by the ability to withstand pain, fatigue, stress, and hardship.

*Significance* - The quality of withstanding pain during a conditioning hike in order to improve stamina is crucial in the development of leadership. Leaders are responsible for leading their units in physical endeavors and for motivating them as well.

*Example* - A Marine keeping up on a 10-mile forced march even though he/she has blisters on both feet.

## 2. 11 LEADERSHIP PRINCIPLES

### Know Yourself and Seek Self Improvement:
- This principle of leadership should be developed by the use of leadership traits. Evaluate yourself by using the leadership traits and determine your strengths and weaknesses.
- You can improve yourself in many ways. To develop the techniques of this principle:
    - Make an honest evaluation of yourself to determine your strong and weak personal qualities
    - Seek the honest opinions of your friends or superiors
    - Learn by studying the causes for the success and failures of others
    - Develop a genuine interest in people
    - Master the art of effective writing and speech
    - Have a definite plan to achieve your goal

### Be Technically and Tactically Proficient:
- A person who knows their job thoroughly and possesses a wide field of knowledge. Before you can lead, you must be able to do the job. Tactical and technical competence can be learned from books and from on the job training. To develop this leadership principle of being technically and tactically proficient, you should:
    - Know what is expected of you then expend time and energy on becoming proficient at those things
    - Form an attitude early on of seeking to learn more than is necessary
    - Observe and study the actions of capable leaders
    - Spend time with those people who are recognized as technically and tactically proficient at those things
    - Prepare yourself for the job of the leader at the next higher rank
    - Seek feedback from superiors, peers and subordinates

### Know Your People and Look Out For Their Welfare:
- This is one of the most important of the leadership principles. A leader must make a conscientious effort to

observe his Marines and how they react to different situations. A Marine who is nervous and lacks self-confidence should never be put in a situation where an important decision must be made. This knowledge will enable you as the leader to determine when close supervision is required.

- To put this principle in to practice successfully you should:
  - Put your Marines' welfare before your own
  - Be approachable
  - Encourage individual development
  - Know your unit's mental attitude; keep in touch with their thoughts
  - Ensure fair and equal distribution of rewards
  - Provide sufficient recreational time and insist on participation

**Keep Your Personnel Informed:**
- Marines by nature are inquisitive. To promote efficiency and morale, a leader should inform the Marines in his unit of all happenings and give reasons why things are to be done. This is accomplished only if time and security permits. Informing your Marines of the situation makes them feel that they are a part of the team and not just a cog in a wheel. Informed Marines perform better.
- The key to giving out information is to be sure that the Marines have enough information to do their job intelligently and to inspire their initiative, enthusiasm, loyalty, and convictions.
- Techniques to apply this principle are:
  - Whenever possible, explain why tasks must be done and the plan to accomplish a task
  - Be alert to detect the spread of rumors. Stop rumors by replacing them with the truth
  - Build morale and XXXpirit de corps by publicizing information concerning successes of your unit
  - Keep your unit informed about current legislation and regulations affecting their pay, promotion, privileges, and other benefits

**Set The Example:**

- A leader who shows professional competence, courage and integrity sets high personal standards for himself before he can rightfully demand it from others. Your appearance, attitude, physical fitness and personal example are all on display daily for the Marines and Sailors in your unit. Remember, your Marines and Sailors reflect your image!
- Techniques for setting the example are to:
    - Show your subordinates that you are willing to do the same things you ask them to do
    - Maintain an optimistic outlook
    - Conduct yourself so that your personal habits are not open to criticism
    - Avoid showing favoritism to any subordinate
    - Delegate authority and avoid over supervision, in order to develop leadership among subordinates
    - Leadership is taught by example

## Ensure That The Task Is Understood, Supervised, and Accomplished:

- Leaders must give clear, concise orders that cannot be misunderstood, and then by close supervision, ensure that these orders are properly executed. Before you can expect your men to perform, they must know what is expected of them.
- The most important part of this principle is the accomplishment of the mission. In order to develop this principle you should:
    - Issue every order as if it were your own
    - Use the established chain of command
    - Encourage subordinates to ask questions concerning any point in your orders or directives they do not understand
    - Question subordinates to determine if there is any doubt or misunderstanding in regard to the task to be accomplished
    - Supervise the execution of your orders
    - Exercise care and thought in supervision; over supervision will hurt initiative and create resentment, while under supervision will not get the job done

## Train Your Marines And Sailors As A Team:

- Teamwork is the key to successful operations. Teamwork is essential from the smallest unit to the entire Marine Corps. As a leader, you must insist on teamwork from your Marines. Train, play and operate as a team. Be sure that each Marine knows his/her position and responsibilities within the team framework.
- To develop the techniques of this principle you should:
    - Stay sharp by continuously studying and training
    - Encourage unit participation in recreational and military events
    - Do not publicly blame an individual for the team's failure or praise just an individual for the team's success
    - Ensure that training is meaningful, and that the purpose is clear to all members of the command
    - Train your team based on realistic conditions
    - Insist that every person understands the functions of the other members of the team and the function of the team as part of the unit

## Make Sound And Timely Decisions:
- The leader must be able to rapidly estimate a situation and make a sound decision based on that estimation. Hesitation or a reluctance to make a decision leads subordinates to lose confidence in your abilities as a leader. Loss of confidence in turn creates confusion and hesitation within the unit.
- Techniques to develop this principle include:
    - Developing a logical and orderly thought process by practicing objective estimates of the situation
    - When time and situation permit planning for every possible event that can reasonably be foreseen
    - Considering the advice and suggestions of your subordinates before making decisions
    - Considering the effects of your decisions on all members of your unit

## Develop A Sense Of Responsibility Among Your Subordinates:
- Another way to show your Marines you are interested in their welfare is to give them the opportunity for professional development. Assigning tasks and delegating

authority promotes mutual confidence and respect between leader and subordinates. It also encourages subordinates to exercise initiative and to give wholehearted cooperation in accomplishment of unit tasks. When you properly delegate authority, you demonstrate faith in your Marines and increase authority, and increase their desire for greater responsibilities.

- To develop this principle you should:
    - Operate through the chain of command
    - Provide clear, well thought out directions
    - Give your subordinates frequent opportunities to perform duties normally performed by more senior personnel
    - Be quick to recognize your subordinates' accomplishments when they demonstrate initiative and resourcefulness
    - Correct errors in judgment and initiative in a way, which will encourage the individual to try harder
    - Give advice and assistance freely when your subordinates request it
    - Resist the urge to micro manage
    - Be prompt and fair in backing subordinates
    - Accept responsibility willingly and insist that your subordinates live by the same standard

## Employ Your Command Within its Capabilities:

- A leader must have a thorough knowledge of the tactical and technical capabilities of the command. Successful completion of a task depends upon how well you know your unit's capabilities. If the task assigned is one that your unit has not been trained to do, failure is very likely to occur. Failures lower your unit's morale and self esteem. Seek out challenging tasks for your unit, but be sure that your unit is prepared for and has the ability to successfully complete the mission.
- Techniques for development of this principle are to:
    - Avoid volunteering your unit for tasks that are beyond their capabilities
    - Be sure that tasks assigned to subordinates are reasonable

- Assign tasks equally among your subordinates
- Use the full capabilities of your unit before requesting assistance

## Seek Responsibilities and Take Responsibility:

- For professional development, you must actively seek out challenging assignments. You must use initiative and sound judgment when trying to accomplish jobs that are required by your grade. Seeking responsibilities also means that you take responsibility for your actions. Regardless of the actions of your subordinates, the responsibility for decisions and their application falls on you.
- Techniques in developing this principle are to:
  - Learn the duties of your immediate senior, and be prepared to accept the responsibilities of these duties
  - Seek a variety of leadership positions that will give you experience in accepting responsibility in different fields
  - Take every opportunity that offers increased responsibility
  - Perform every task, no matter whether it is top secret or seemingly trivial, to the best of your ability
  - Stand up for what you think is right. Have courage in your convictions
  - Carefully evaluate a subordinate's failure before taking action against that subordinate
  - In the absence of orders, take the initiative to perform the actions you believe your senior would direct you to perform if present

End excerpt.

Between the Principles and Traits listed above and the short description I gave about leadership immediately prior, you should be developing a pretty clear picture of what Marine Corps leadership is.

Throughout your career you'll attend school after school to master all of the above. The truth is that, at some point, you'll have to become comfortable enough with Marine Corps leadership principles and traits that you can integrate them into your own personality. This point is usually where problems arise.

As I said before, there are few, if any, natural born leaders. Often, when we begin to learn about Marine Corps leadership and start to put it into practice, we don't do it perfectly. The traits and principles themselves are perfect, but when they are tinged by personality, they become something very unique to the individual Marine.

A Marine who is incorporating these principles and traits into their lifestyle will make mistakes. Some Marines will always make mistakes and will never become good leaders. Some of them will take to leadership like a duck to water. Regardless of how easily you adapt the leadership traits and principles into your life, you will make mistakes and you will have to work at it.

The flip-side of that coin is that YOUR leaders are doing the same thing. They are learning as they gain experience, just as you will. So, try to have some consideration for this fact when things happen that you don't like. Remember that there are about 15 levels of leaders between you and the Commandant of the Marine Corps. Not every one of those 15 Marines is going to be great at what they do every day. Try to be a little understanding that we are all human and sometimes we fuck up.

**The primary mission(s) of Marine Corps leadership is 1) mission accomplishment and 2) troop welfare.** A great way to become a really good leader of Marines is to watch your leaders closely. Watch everything they do and take note of the things that are effective, take note of the things that are not effective (or counterproductive), take note of the things they do that you really hate, then take note of the things they do that you really like. Then, reflect on all the things they did and evaluate them against the 2 goals of leadership. Ask yourself if the things your leaders did were productive toward mission accomplishment, or if they were productive toward troop welfare.

This is a little easier said than done because a lot of these things happen during periods of operational intensity. Also, as a Marine being led, you aren't always privy to all the information that your leaders are given. Regardless, always try to go back over every operational period with a critical mind. Operational reflection is something the Marine Corps as a whole does formally and frequently in order to improve techniques, tactics and procedures. They call it "lessons learned". Shouldn't you also reflect on the leadership you observe as a learning exercise?

If you actually do this exercise, you'll start to see things that your leaders do in a different light. You'll start to realize that some things they do that you hated were for the benefit of mission accomplishment or even for your benefit; or some things they do that you really liked were for the benefit of troop welfare. You'll even notice times when leadership decisions didn't serve either the mission or troop welfare, and that they may have only served the leader or his/her ego (yes, it happens).

Whatever the case, if you understand that mission accomplishment and troop welfare are the only legitimate objectives, you'll automatically begin to evaluate your leaders and your own decisions with a far more rational and military mind. This really is the first big step to becoming a really good leader of Marines, or anyone else.

At this point I'd like to interject one thing: **You don't have to be an ass-hole to be a good leader.** In fact, ass-holes seldom make good leaders. I've seen many would-be leaders treat Marines like complete shit, just because they can. Worse, I've seen leaders make decisions that adversely affect the personal welfare of a Marine and that Marines family, not for the purpose of mission accomplishment, but because that was the decision the leader made, and by god, that leader was going to stick to it! So, if you EVER make a decision that doesn't benefit mission accomplishment and/or troop welfare, you need to immediately re-evaluate your decision. The odds are that you made that decision for your own convenience, and if that's the case, you've just fucked up.

Why am I asking you to look at your leaders' decisions critically? Because that can only help you develop your own decision making process. Watching a senior Marine make a decision that screws everyone over for no real operational benefit, is a great opportunity to make sure YOU never make that mistake when you're leading Marines. So, take advantage of this. It's like having a free how-to video (or how-not-to) of your very own to learn from. Don't let those opportunities go to waste.

Please be aware that I didn't bring all this up so that you can run around questioning every order that you are given. **Marines instantly and willingly obey all lawful orders they are given without hesitation**. The ONLY TIME you should ever question an order is if it's something that will violate the laws of war or the UCMJ. You can bet that if you receive an order that violates either the UCMJ or the Laws of War that it's not going to be a lawful one. So, I said all that to say: Don't be a dumbass sea-lawyer who thinks every other order you get is unlawful. Join the Navy if you want to play that game.

Once you've gotten a good handle on the Marine Corps leadership principles and traits, the next big step is to understand the leadership process and the function of a "Commanders Intent". Commanders Intent is just that, the intent of a commander regarding a specific issue or objective, or the intended outcome. Every commander should ALWAYS inform his/her troops about his/her intent regarding anything his/her troops will work toward. If it's important enough to do, it's important enough to make known the commanders intent.

When a commander tells Marines what his/her intent is, those Marines now know what the desired outcome is. This gives the Marines the knowledge and flexibility they need to adjust their operational activities as a situation develops. This is the secret to Marine Corps leadership, and why it will always be superior to other forms of leadership (in my opinion).

It's commonly known that, when bullets start flying, whatever plan you had often goes out the window. When that happens, if your Marines understand the intended outcome of their action, they can form a new plan to achieve the same result and put it in play immediately, instead of calling back to a commander for instructions (which is what lesser forms of leadership demand). Marines that know the Commanders Intent can act dynamically, retain the initiative, and more easily force their collective will upon the enemy while they are calling back to the rear asking permission to adjust.

When you are in charge of Marines, always remember to relay to them the commanders' intent. If you fail to pass that word to your Marines, you are doing your Marines a dis-service, and you might as well be in the Army, or some other force that is crippled with oversight and micro-management.

History is peppered with stories of young warriors that have found themselves cut off from their leadership, with no guidance on an evolving battlefield. Those warriors that understand the commanders' intent can still do something to effect the outcome of a battle, even if they are alone with no guidance… but ONLY if they understand the bigger picture, and that means knowing the commanders intent. I recommend you read the book "Message to Garcia" for a perfect example of this. It's a short book and an easy read, but the message about Commanders' Intent is in there, and it is fucking important!

The bottom line with all this leadership stuff is that you are being groomed to be a leader starting the day you become a recruit, and continue being groomed for higher leadership responsibility until the day you get out. You are going to have some GREAT leaders to look up to in the Marine Corps, I guarantee it! I've met some that seemed almost super-human. Just understand that they learned to behave like that somewhere along the way, and you can too!

You will also meet your share of complete douche-bags that are more concerned about themselves than anything else. Of those douche-bags that try to make the Marine Corps a career, I've noticed that most of those guys tend to stall out around the SSgt/GySgt rank on the enlisted side (if they get that high at all), and the Capt/Maj rank on the officer side (again, thankfully most of them don't make it that far). These people serve a good purpose as great examples of what not to do. Hopefully you'll be able to learn from them in a safe, garrison environment. Learning from people like this in a combat zone is hazardous; maybe not hazardous to you, but definitely hazardous to someone, and usually not the enemy.

Last thing I have for you on leadership is, don't ever stop learning, adapting and evolving your leadership skills. Your welfare and the welfare of your Marines depend on you being a good student of leadership throughout your career. I don't care if you're a SgtMaj or a Col, none of us know everything, and none of us are perfect… we can only strive to be.

# 9 STUFF YOU NEED TO KNOW BEFORE YOU HIT THE FLEET

I was originally going to call this chapter "Equal Opportunity",

but then realized that everyone would likely skip this chapter if I did

that. Instead, I'm filling this chapter with **shit you need to know** to

be successful.

**Item number 1**: There are people in the Marine Corps that are

different than you. If you can't treat other people with dignity and

respect regardless of what color, gender or religion, ethnic group or

sexual orientation they are, don't join.

**Item number 2**: Female Marines are an extreme minority in the

Corps. They are Marines, not personal play toys for male Marines.

They deserve to be treated exactly the same as any other Marine.

Failing to treat them the same is an insult to them and unfair to their

male peers.

**Item number 3**: If you are a female Marine, you are a Marine. You deserve, and will get the same opportunities as any other Marine (with only a few exceptions for some direct combat roles, as of 2012). DO NOT try to use your gender to try to gain special favors from other Marines. It's not fucking right, and once you do that you will be labeled for the rest of your career (no joke). Not only that, but after you do something like that, every other female Marine in your unit will have a harder time getting even the most basic respect from other Marines, all because you chose to manipulate others for your own gain. No amount of discretion is going to keep that sort of thing under wraps either, so just don't do it.

**Item number 4**: Marines are "steely-eyed killers", but that doesn't mean we get to behave like barbarians. We are professional warriors. We take prisoners. We treat prisoners humanely. We treat the wounded, on both sides. We care for those that can't care for themselves. We are polite and well mannered. We play hard, but within the bounds of the law. We work hard, always giving our maximum effort. We fight hard, as long as we have a means to fight. We don't leave other Marines behind. We kill enemy combatants with extreme, overwhelming firepower and maneuver.

**Item number 5**: We do not "initiate" or "haze" other Marines into our units. Marines only experience one initiation, and that's the receipt of their Eagle, Globe and Anchor during boot camp. We do not try to cause pain, discomfort or injury to our fellow Marines in the name of "pinning", "Hazing", "initiating", or during periods of drunken stupidity.

**Item number 6**: We do not refer to other people in racial terms like "slope", "nigga", "kike", "Sand-nigger", "cracker", "chink", "wet-back", etc (there are a million of them, and none of them are appropriate). I don't care if you're friends with the other person or not, or if you're of African-American decent and using the "N" word toward another African-American Marine. These terms are offensive, unbecoming and the ONLY acceptable use of terms like these are for legitimate training purposes (which is what I consider this book).

**Item number 7**: The legal drinking age in the Marine Corps is 21. If you're not 21, don't drink. If you do, you will get caught and punished. If you're in a country where the drinking age is less than 21, look to your commander for guidance on drinking. If there is a waiver for the 21 year old drinking age, that info will be available from the commander, and you can bet it will be made known.

**Item number 8**: We are always willing to do extra work, and we are always on time (In the Marine Corps, 15 minutes early = on time, but 15 minutes early to be 15 minutes early is fucking stupid, unless your showing up at a place that operates on a first come, first served basis).

The truth is that the population of the Marine Corps is fed by the population of the United States. Therefore, logic dictates that the Marine Corps population should be at least somewhat similar to the population of the US, right? Well, not quite. For example, about half the US population is female. The female Marine Corps population is only about 6% of the total USMC active Marine population. Approximately 15% of the US population is of African American origin, but African Americans make up only 10% of the Marine Corps (as of 2011). Other most recent demographic numbers on active duty are: Hispanic: 12.6%, American Indian, Alaskan Native, Asian, Pacific Islander, or Declined to Respond: 7.2% (as of 2011). Nearly all ethnicities are represented in the Marine Corps, but the weight of each ethnicity is different than we find in daily civilian life, especially when it comes to gender.

I hope that there's a little voice in your head asking, "Why the hell should I care about this? Working with people of other races, religions or gender makes absolutely no difference to me". I would expect anyone with even a little education to feel that way. That opinion generally reflects the values of our country, I think. Everyone is welcome; you won't be judged based on where you came from, the color of your skin or how much money your family has; each of us has value and can contribute to the greater good; everyone should be treated with dignity and respect, right?

The reality is that this is the current culture of the United States. This all inclusive culture has been directed to permeate through the Department of Defense, and by extension, through the Marine Corps. Therefore, our Marines Corps is a Corps that any able bodied person can serve in.

Why am I saying all this? I'm saying this because there are people in our country that don't believe everyone is equal. There are people in our country who are racists, bigots, sexists, homophobes or just un-educated chuckle-heads that hate people that are different than themselves, pretty much just because they are different. There are others that think women should be barefoot and pregnant at home, taking care of the cooking, laundry and kids. There are still others that don't think they have any prejudice toward anyone, but they have a deep-seated belief that certain things should be a certain way.

Whatever the case, as a Marine, you will be stressed and worked hard in confined places under crappy circumstances and miserable conditions. The last thing anyone is going to need in situations like that are some idiots that can't seem to accept that they have to take orders from an African American, Hispanic or female Marine. Most people that can't get over stupid little issues like that tend to be weeded out in boot camp, but sometimes they still make it through.

Most recently, Congress passed a law that allows gay men and women to openly serve in the Military. This comes at a time when the country is generally pushing for the acceptance of gay people, but not everyone is on board with that idea quiet yet. So, if you have a problem with gay men or women, you're going to need to overcome that problem and learn how to treat everyone with the same respect and dignity that you'd treat your brother or your sister with. If you can't, don't join.

I'm going to break down some of this ethnic diversity stuff into ironically segregated sections for ease of consumption, so I can elaborate a bit on some specific things.

**Race**: Our country has a tumultuous history when it comes to racial relations. We have experienced tension between citizens and immigrants; between immigrants of one nationality against immigrants of another nationality; between Americans of one national origin against Americans of another national origin; between northern Americans and southern slave-holding Americans; between Caucasian Americans and African Americans; between Americans and Native Americans; between Americans and Chinese immigrants, many of them former slaves (during the 1800's); between Americans and German Americans (during WWI and WWII); between Americans and Japanese Americans (during WWII); between Americans and middle-eastern Americans (2001 -2010); between conservative American Christians and American Atheists; between homophobic Americans and Gay Americans (ongoing).

For Christ sake! Our country was founded by immigrants. Who the fuck are we to treat other immigrants badly? Our founders were people that were trying to escape religious persecution. You would think that by now, some 500 years later, we would have gotten over all this. Well, sometimes it takes time to get it right. After all, those same people that wanted to escape religious persecution started buying slaves at some point, didn't they?

So, the point here is that we all come from different places and different walks of life. We are certainly living in a more enlightened time than any other time in history. All people generally agree that they should treat their own family with compassion, respect and dignity. So, as a Marine, you will be charged with treating all Marines with respect and dignity, and as a leader, you should find a place for compassion, just as you might for your own children.

That's really the point of all the Equal Opportunity talk anyway, isn't it? Treating people with respect and dignity and a little compassion? It is a pretty simple concept, I think. So why, then, have I dedicated a chapter of my book on Marine Corps Success to this subject? The answer is that there are people out there that still just don't get it.

The Marine Corps has Equal Opportunity officers because there is a need for them. Occasionally a racial issue does come up, and it's Marine Corps policy (at least at the time I'm writing this) to handle them swiftly and fairly in order to correct any injustices and get everyone focused back on the mission. During my brief time as an Equal Opportunity Program Manager, I noticed that the majority of the issues had to do with either gender or general unfair treatment (not necessarily involving race). In fact, I was surprised that I had so few instances involving race compared to the other instances.

Here is an example of something I saw happen during my time as a Marine Leader. Please read it and think about what you would do if you were the immediate supervisor of the Cpl involved.

Case Study 1:

A young Cpl working for a Marine aviation Detachment one day, goes on Facebook in his barracks room and posts several comments about his African American male MSgt. The MSgt was the SNCOIC of the Detachment, and the Cpl apparently had some sort of a personality conflict with him. So, Cpl Numb-nutz posts a bunch of hateful comments on his Facebook profile about his MSgt, stating that he's a (N-word) this and a (N-word) that. Of course, Cpl Numb-nutz has several platoon members that are linked to his Facebook account, as well as a few SNCO's.

One of the SNCO's had an exchange with Cpl Numb-nutz over Facebook, then notified the Squadron EO Marine, a SSgt. After that it was all over for Cpl Numb-nutz. Here's why: you can't go around calling other Marines hateful, racist names because that's detrimental to good order and discipline... oh, and a Cpl was being EXTREMELY disrespectful to a MSgt. That alone was enough to NJP that idiot. To make matters worse, he apparently had some dislike for African Americans, making that stupid little rant not just disrespectful, but outright hateful propaganda. So, Cpl Numb-nutz had a shorter than expected career with the Marines. As far as I'm concerned, his departure wasn't soon enough. End case study.

**Gender:**

Most of the EO issues I've run across during my career have had to do with gender. Don't make the mistake of thinking that "gender" is the problem. Gender is only a common factor in a number of problems that I've seen. I think the REAL problem is that many men have no idea how to treat a woman equally.... just my opinion, of course.

So, here's how to treat a woman as an equal: treat her like she's your brother or any other person who might be a co-worker that you have NO ITENTION or desire of having a sexual relationship with. That's pretty simple, right? It's not always easy to do, but it's an absolute necessity! If you fuck this up, the consequences are always messy, and often extremely damaging to career, family and your unit.

On the other hand, if you're a female Marine, you should treat other Marines like they are your brother or any other person who might be a co-worker that you have NO ITENTION or desire of having a sexual relationship with. The difference is that women have to deal with some men that have so little experience working with women that they tend to trip all over their own dicks when talking to one. This is where temptation must be put in check. When talking to a Marine with this problem (and it'll be obvious that he has it), you've got to be extremely professional. You cannot "flirt" with a man like this and expect to have a normal relationship after that. Men like this are idiots, and occasionally need to be reminded of everyone's purpose.

One little trick I've heard is effective for helping men treat women as equals was recently relayed me. This young woman showed up at a new duty station to check into a barracks room and immediately started receiving "cat calls" from the barracks. She jumped in her car, drove to the nearest pawn shop and bought an engagement ring. She went back to the barracks, moved in, and had few problems after that. So, if you're a female Marine, this might help you too.

Case Study 2:

I was a Corporal (Platoon Sergeant) with a platoon of Marines. While conducting a field day in the barracks, I went through each room as the Marines were cleaning, to point out some areas to pay special attention to. At the time I was a Field Radio Operator, and a few weeks before we'd just received the first two female Radio Operators that I'd ever met. They were fresh out of school and they roomed together in the same hallway as all the other Marines.

I entered their room to do the same as I did for everyone else, but I was confronted with the two of them standing there with no shirts on (bra's were in place) holding their hair up and one of them asked, "Do we look better with our hair up like this, or down, in these shorts?' Apparently they were wearing some silkies too, but I was so shocked that I didn't notice. I yelled something to this effect, "Put some god-damned shirts on, clean this fucking pig-style of a room and DON'T YOU EVER FUCKING DO THAT TO ME AGAIN! DO YOU UNDERSTAND?" I was pissed off because those two young Marines tried to compromise my leadership of the platoon by pulling that on me. They probably didn't see it that way. They probably thought it was "harmless", but it was my job to set them strait, so that's what I tried to do.

End case study.

I never had a problem with either of them again, although it should be noted that one of them eventually ended up in a relationship with another Cpl in the Admin shop. He was married to someone else.

The last thing I want to touch on regarding gender is what I like to call "Stupid Old Man Disease". When I was coming up as a NCO and SNCO, I noticed that many of my senior enlisted male Marines totally changed their demeanor in front of female Marines. I noticed it as a Cpl, but as I was promoted and grew through the ranks it seem almost as if it were an epidemic! Luckily, during my last 5 years in the

Corps, this trend seemed to be disappearing, but I'm still blown away to this day by some of the stuff I saw senior enlisted leaders do.

Case Study 3:

MSgt So-and-so is working in a headquarters sections next to many other "S" shops with many other senior and junior Marines. MSgt So-and-so notices a young LCpl that joins the unit, LCpl Hard-Charger. Months later LCpl Hard-Charger gets promoted to Cpl. MSgt So-and-so notices Cpl Hard-Charger leaving work late from work one Friday and follows her out the door. Thinking that after hours on a Friday no one would be around, MSgt So-and-so stops Cpl Hard-Charger as she's backing out of the parking lot. She rolls down her window to ask what the MSgt wants. The MSgt makes up some excuse for stopping her then leans into her car and tries to stick his tongue down her throat!

Cpl Hard-Charger, having none of this, pushes him away and drives away. That weekend, all she can do is think about how upsetting that was. She works right across the hall from that MSgt's office. How can she go to work and look him in the face again? What will he say when she sees him? How will he act towards her?

MSgt So-and-so apparently had no problem being rejected. He went home to his wife and kids, then came to work the next Monday like nothing happened.

That Sunday night Cpl Hard-Charger was really getting anxious about the next day. She was becoming more and more uncomfortable with the whole situation and really needed some advice. It turns out that Cpl Hard-Charger's SNCO, a female GySgt, use to be the unit's Sexual Assault Response Coordinator (SARC). Cpl Hard-Charger called GySgt SARC on Sunday night to talk about the situation.

The Equal Opportunity (EO) Marine for this unit was a MSgt and was on TAD, but was due back the next day. After talking with Cpl Hard-Charger, GySgt SARC called the unit Executive Officer (XO) to inform him of the issue. The next day the unit EO returned. The XO called him into the office and asked him to investigate the allegation. The EO did so. He spoke with Cpl Hard-Charger, then he spoke with MSgt So-and-so. MSgt So-and-so completely lost it during the interview. He was immediately aware of what he had done wrong and was very concerned about the ramifications of his actions, even though he was retiring within the year.

As it turned out, the EO was able to find a satisfactory solution for all parties concerned, and the issue was put to rest without further involvement from the command, or higher authority. What was the resolution? The EO MSgt told MSgt So-and-so to stay the fuck away from Cpl Hard-Charger, and that failure to do so would result in MSgt So-and-so receiving a nice NJP or Courts Martial as a parting gift for his retirement.

End case study.

So, as you can see, sometimes senior Marines have errors in judgment. Thankfully, in this case, we found a resolution that worked with as little pain to the parties and the command as possible, but it doesn't always work out that way.

In fact, I've often seen things like this come up, and seen the first reaction of the command being moving the Cpl out of her shop into another office, far away from the MSgt. As far as I'm concerned, moving the VICTIM of an advance like this instead of moving the OFFENDER, is a gross injustice. Why should Cpl Hard-Charger be inconvenienced and made to feel like she's being punished when MSgt So-and-so is the one that's a douche-bag? If someone has to be moved, move the offender, otherwise you risk losing all sense of justice by the young Marines in the unit.

Yes, I was the EO MSgt in this story.

Last case study:

This'll be a short one. I was sitting on a Squadron/Battalion level meritorious promotion board around 1999. I was a SSgt. The board was being run by our unit SgtMaj. This was a particularly unusual board, because the SgtMaj requested that NCO's sit on the board with him, instead of the usual complement of GySgt's and above. It was a meritorious promotion board for LCpl and Cpl, and he thought it would be a good idea for our NCO's to pick the newest addition to their ranks.

So, I'm the only other SNCO in the room, and the SgtMaj starts the board by explaining how it would work to the NCO's. I've been a party to many boards by this time, so this process was nothing new to me.

We had 5 LCpl's competing for one Meritorious Cpl promotion. Four of them were male Marines, one was a female Marine. The female Marine apparently worked in the Admin shop (S-1) and the other Marines came from other various parts of the unit.

The board went along as normal. The 4 male Marines came in, one at a time. Most of them were pretty average as far as general knowledge, many of them had great scores on their annual qualifications, but one of them was quite good. He had some of the highest scores, had one hell of a sharp uniform and he only missed 1 out of the 21 general knowledge questions we asked him. Pretty impressive, I thought.

The female LCpl came in last. Her uniform looked fine, but she only answer 3 out of 21 questions correctly and her military bearing was not good (her eyeballs and head were all over the place). At one point, she actually rolled her eyes when asked a question she clearly didn't know. Her scores and other competitive documentation were unimpressive.

When she stepped out, we all began discussing everyone's performance. Shockingly, the first thing that was said when the she left the room was this: "Wow, that young lady sure had her shit together! Wasn't she great?" the SgtMaj said as he looked in my direction.

I was speechless. Sitting on the SgtMaj's right, I scanned the faces of the NCO's in the room. They were all looking at me to see what I'd say. I turned back to the SgtMaj and said, "What Board were you sitting on, SgtMaj? That Marines' bearing was all over the place and she didn't know her ass from a hole in the ground."

The SgtMaj then looked to each NCO for input. Most of them didn't know what to say. They didn't want to say anything against the SgtMaj's opinion, but they knew he was way off the mark on the female LCpl's performance. We talked it out, the whole time the SgtMaj did his best to convince each NCO that LCpl Hole-in-the-ground was the best Marine for the promotion. I fought back as respectfully as posible and we ended up promoting the male Marines that had great scores, great knowledge and a sharp look.

Although there was no monkey-business going on between the SgtMaj and LCpl Hole-in-the-ground (that I know of), the SgtMaj's obvious familiarity with her clearly colored his opinion of her performance. If he'd have had his way, she would have been meritoriously promoted instead of that hard-core LCpl that was doing everything right and performing at the higher level.

End case study.

Now, let me ask you a few things: If you were an NCO sitting on this board, how would you have felt? If LCpl Hole-in-the-ground were promoted that day and you were that hard-core LCpl that competed against her, how would you have felt? I can't answer those questions for you, or for those NCO's that sat on the board with me, but I can say that I was pretty pissed off when I walk out of that board room.

I was totally disgusted at what the SgtMaj had done. For fuck-sake, was the SgtMaj so smitten with this young lady that he didn't realize how blatantly he was trying to favor her? Did he not realize that the moral of every NCO in that room (and every NCO in the unit, once the board members left that room… peers talk, especially when they're pissed) was in danger of being torpedoed? The most appropriate acronym in my mind at the time was (WTF?).

My SgtMaj clearly had a raging case of SOMD that day, and I've seen many, many, many other senior leaders develop the same disease. So, be mindful of the behavior of others. If you're a female Marine, you'll see this happen to you. It'll be tempting to accept more favorable treatment from people like this, but try to resist. Things like this aren't your fault as a female Marine, but it's still not right.

**Hazing**:

Hazing is when someone who has already been through something (like boot camp, joining a new unit, getting promoted to a new rank, getting "jump" wings, etc.) makes another Marine, who is newly going through the same thing, perform some stupid "ritual" or "tradition" in which they are subjected to pain, injury or humiliation.

The Marine Corps/Commandants policy on hazing is that it is "Not Tolerated" in any form. I came up with hazing. I was hazed left and right. I was expected to haze others. This was all before hazing was banned in the mid 1990's. Each time I was hazed or was expected to haze someone, it was not a pleasant thing. Everyone I've ever seen hazed didn't enjoy it. I didn't enjoy getting my "Blood Stripes", and I didn't enjoy being "promoted" by 4 platoons of Marines when I picked up PFC. In fact, I only remember the first 4 hits, after that everything is a blank for me. Judging by the swelling in my arms and shoulders afterward, I'm pretty sure I was hit by all 83 of them. Some Marines have actually been hospitalized, maimed, medically discharged and even killed because some dick-head decided to haze them.

Hazing another Marine is the ultimate in disrespect. If you do it, you deserve to be beaten within an inch of your life, as far as I'm concerned. Here are some examples of hazing that I've seen. If you hear of someone considering doing any of these or anything that even sounds like these, stop them before someone gets hurt, or gets a court-martial:

- "Pinning" during or after a promotion. Includes punching promotees, driving their new chevrons into their collar bones, kneeing a new Cpl in the legs, or striking newly promoted Marines anywhere on the body.

- Initiating new Marines. This could be making them run around looking for fictional objects like "flight-line", "prop-wash", "frequency grease", "BA-1100n's", "ID-10-T forms", "registering an Arty round", and many other stupid errands whose only purpose is humiliation. Other forms of initiation are often physical like, forcing someone to binge drink, duct-taping a Marine to a board, fence, HMMWV hood or whatever for an extended

period, using a Marine as a battering ram, or forcing any
Marine to participate in any other form of hazing… etc.

- Atomic sit-ups. (Don't ask)

- "Ax Qualifying". Note: we don't qualify with blades in the
Marines.

- Any form of "Incentive training" after boot camp.

- "Punishing" a Marine for some indiscretion. Note: Only
one person in your unit has the authority to "punish" a
Marine, and that is your Commanding Officer.


Anyway, you get the idea. One more thing that is a huge no-no is
screwing with someone that is unconscious or unable to defend
themselves. Examples: Finding a friend unconscious and/or drunk
and: writing on their face with a permanent marker, shaving their
head, "tea-bagging" them while taking pictures, and so on.

The days of hazing are over and they have been for a long time.
Don't screw around with those type of activities, and if you see
someone doing them, stop them, then kick them in the balls for
being an asshole. The only place that crap happens any more is in
third rate colleges.

## 10 MONEY

You're probably wondering why I'm including a chapter on money in this book. Most people think that military people are poorly paid. I think that's still true, but in recent years the pay has increased nicely to at least try to bring military pay close to civilian world pay.

The reason for this chapter is because I had a very rude awakening during my 12<sup>th</sup> year on active duty. I was assigned an additional billet as the unit "Command Finance Specialist". The first order of business in that position was going to an MCCS sponsored Command Finance Specialist course, in which we learned how to teach people to make a budget and balance a check book.

During that course I was given a book that lit a fire in my belly to learn more about money. I ravenously read as many books about money that I could get my hands on over the next 3 years. I read 300 books on the subject before I stopped counting. I began teaching young Marines about money whenever I could spare the time, and eventually became a strong advocate of financial literacy. You'll see why in a minute.

So, why then am I bringing this subject to you? I'm telling you about this for four reasons. 1) The only financial advice I ever got from my parents was, "Save your money". That little pearl of wisdom was fucking useless. 2) Once I went to college I realized that they don't teach financial anything in college unless you're studying to be in the finance business. This seems ridiculous to me, since MONEY is needed by every American just to survive. 3) Once I learned about money, I realized what a deep and important subject it was for me and everyone else, and became appalled that, as important as money seems to be to our survival, no public schools teach anything about it beyond counting money and figuring future interest rates in your high school algebra class. Lastly, 4) Marines don't make shit compared to many civilian technical jobs, and it pisses me off to no end that a Marine can give his or her entire adult life to the service of our country and the Corps, only to be cast aside like a used candy wrapper, with a very meager life savings, if any.

So, I'm writing this chapter to show you how you can retire from the Corps as a millionaire after 20 years of service. Did I do that? No. I learned about this stuff too late. But you can if you start IMMEDIATELY!

Let's talk about numbers and compounded interest. Did you know that the stock market has averaged a return of about 11% per year since the 1920's? Most people thinking about a Marine Corps career couldn't give two shits about the stock market, believe me, I know. BUT THIS IS IMPORTANT, SO PAY ATTENTION! That's 11% each year on the average, during a time period when we had 1 depression, at least 2 major recessions, a world war and 2 long and expensive wars in Viet Nam and the "War on Terror"! 11% per year for 90+ years! That's a pretty good indication that the 11% return is something that can reasonable be relied upon to continue, unless something catastrophic like the apocalypse happens, and then we won't be needing money anyway. This should tell you that a very average investor should be able to make 11% annually no matter what… all they have to do is invest in the market. I'll explain how later.

You have $100 in 1920 and you invest it in the stock market. 1

year from then your $100 has turned into $111. In 1930, you'd have

$283.94. Today your $100 would have turned into $1,478,134.82, and

3 years from now that $100 will have increased to $2,021,543.01!

So, $100 invested for 95 years at an average return of 11% yields

over $2 million dollars today. Great! That doesn't mean shit to you,

right? Wrong.


Let's imagine that today we start investing. Instead of investing

one small amount and letting it sit for a century, let's see what's really

possible for the average person that isn't already rich. As I write this,

base pay in the Marine Corps as an E-1 is $1516 per month based on

the 2013 pay tables. Let's say that, after getting out of boot camp, you

decide to invest. If you're not married, this is the perfect time to do

it, because you probably have very few bills. You live in the barracks.

You're fed at the chow hall. The only thing you need to spend your

money on is maintaining your uniforms, and you get an annual

allowance for that too! So, clearly someone in this position has

money coming in that they can start building their future with.

We have $1516 per month of income with no real bills. Let's say we invest 1/3 of our income, and use the rest for having fun and buying things we don't really need. Watch how this plays out.

You invest $505 every month for 5 years. After 5 years of deposits and returns of 11%, you have $38,086.43. Let's let that money sit in the same account and continue to collect interest until we get to 20 years. Now we're going to stop putting $505 into that investment, and start a new one. You've been promoted 4 times in 5 years and now you're a Sgt earning $2530 per month. Other than your investments, you've wasted every dime you've made on gadgets, clothes and dating. Now, with the new promotion, you decide it's time to increase your investment plan back to the original 1/3 of your income.

You set up a new investment allotment in the amount of $843.33 (1/3 of a Sgt's base pay as of 2013) into an investment that will return you 11%. For the next 5 years that amount automatically goes into your investment. At the end of 5 years this second investment is now worth $63602.83. Your first investment has continued to grow and is now worth $64177.85. Congratulations, you're a hundred-thousand-aire! Now you do the same thing. Slide investment #2 onto the shelf, stop putting money into it, and just allow it to continue making money. Now we start investment number 3.

It's your 10 year mark in the Marines. You're a SSgt and your base pay is now $3298 (based on 2013 pay chart. Your actual pay will be higher.) You've shelved investment #2 and are now ready to create investment #3. You're married now. No kids yet and the wife has an income. We can still make 1/3 of your pay work and you begin investing $1099.33 per month into the market and realize a nice, steady 11% return. In 5 years that investment has grown to $82910.01. Investment number 2 continued to grow and it's now worth $107174.47, and investment number 1 is worth $108143.41.

It's year 15. You're a GySgt now. You shelve investment #3 and start #4 based on your GySgt income of $4044 per month. 1/3 of this is $1348. You set up the allotment for $1348 and let it ride for 5 years, at the end of which it's grown to $101664.37. Meanwhile investment #1 is now worth $182227.93, investment #2 is now worth $180595.21, and investment #3 is now worth $139708.19. You're at 20 years in the Marines and you now have a nice nest-egg of $604,195.70 to show for it. Not bad! That should last you a while if you'd like to get out at 20 and find a normal job.

If you let this amount ride for beyond retirement while your start your second career, here's what it'll be worth:

5 years after retirement:      $1,018,104.89

10 years after retirement:     $1,716,565.95

20 years after retirement:     $4,871,213.96

30 years after retirement:     $13,831,427.15

40 years after retirement:     $39,273,244.52

Assuming you joined at age 18 and followed my program to the letter, you'd be sitting on top of a pile of cash at the age of 78, to the tune of just over $39 million dollars. This will allow you to spend your 80's in comfort, I'd say.

This is a very easy-to-implement strategy, costing you only a little time and the money you put into it. You don't have to learn much at all about stocks and investing. You just need to learn how to find an EFT (Exchange Traded Fund) that follows whichever stock market index you'd prefer to invest in. In other words, one that follows the Dow Jones Industrial, the S&P 500, or the NASDAQ. Just to help you understand these a little better, Dow Jones tracks large companies that have been around forever (probably your best bet),

S&P 500 tracks more "mid-cap" companies that are still big, but are smaller than the giants. These companies may have a shorter track record and may be a little more volatile. Then the NASDAQ contains a bunch of technology oriented stocks. These tend to have a much shorter track record, plus many of these companies could be gone 2 years from now due to replacement by a better technology.

You're best chance of achieving that average 11% return is by going with the giants that live on the Dow Jones list because most of these are the stocks that have been around for the last 100 years and performed at the 11% I mentioned. These companies should be the most stable and have the most consistent growth over longer periods.

Everything I just told you in the previous 4 pages is enough for you to make this happen, starting now. Do it now. Don't wait, or believe me, you'll find yourself at 41 years old looking back with no real investments wondering how that time flew by so damn fast.

If you're a sports fan, particularly a football fan, you probably already know about the problem that many former NFL players are having now. Although their pay was lower a few decades ago, many of them chose to spend their money instead of investing it. Today, former NFL players that were once making a few million dollars a year are now broke and living off a meager retirement. They chose to "live for today" and now they're fucked and living in squalor. Do you want that for yourself? For your kids?

All it takes is just a little bit of effort. Set up an investment account for yourself and get a simple plan like this going. Once it's on autopilot, you don't have to think about it again until your pay changes. There's no stress or worrying about stocks and the economy, because we have a 90 year track record of reasonable returns even through some of the worst periods in our nation's history.

How would you like to be a little more than an average investor? If an average investor can make 11% annually, what do you think a better-than-average investor could make? Since I don't know many Marines that like to be average, I'll tell you.

Warren Buffett is considered by many to be one of the all-time greatest investors ever. He did it through his companies, but he's managed to earn over 20% annually since 1968. He's not the only one that has done that, but he is the most public figure that has a great investment record.

Warren Buffett's investment strategy is pretty simple, and reasonably easy to learn. I'll show you where to learn it shortly. First, let's look at the returns we might get if you invested like Mr. Buffet did.

Same scenario as before: We join the Marines and intend to invest 1/3 of our income throughout our career, or at least as long as we can stand to live on 2/3's of our base pay. This is a lot easier to do if you aren't married. If you are married, it's easier to do if your spouse is employed and you don't have kids. If you have kids, it's easier to do if your spouse works too. If you're divorced with kids, you might have to get a second job to make this work. Either way, this is what it might look like...

You read 3 books that I mention at the end of this chapter and learn how to invest like a champ. You get good at it (it's not that hard... really!) and you manage to pull an average 19% return throughout your 20 years on active duty. We have $1516 per month of income with no real bills. Let's say we invest 1/3 of our income, and use the rest for having fun and buying things we don't really need.

You invest $505 every month for 5 years. After 5 years of deposits and returns of 19%, you have $44917.49. Let's let that money sit in the same account and continue to collect interest until we get to 20 years. Now we're going to stop putting $505 into that investment, and start a new one. You've been promoted 4 times in 5 years and now you're a Sgt earning $2530 per month. Other than your investments, you've wasted every dime you've made on gadgets, clothes and dating. Now, with the new promotion, you decide it's time to increase your investment plan back to the original 1/3 of your income.

You set up a new investment allotment in the amount of $843.33 (1/3 of a Sgt's base pay as of 2013) into an investment that will return you 19%. For the next 5 years that amount automatically goes into your investment. At the end of 5 years this second investment is now worth $75010.44. Your first investment has continued to grow and is now worth $107189.02. Now you slide investment #2 onto the shelf, stop putting money into it, and just allow it to continue making money. Now we start investment number 3.

It's your 10 year mark in the Marines. You're a SSgt and your base pay is now $3298 (based on 2013 pay chart. Your actual pay will be higher.) You're married now. No kids yet and the spouse has an income. We can still make 1/3 of your pay work and you begin investing $1099.33 per month into a great investment and realize a nice 19% return. In 5 years that investment has grown to $97780.49. Investment number 2 continued to grow and it's now worth $179001.44, and investment number 1 is worth $255790.90. What's it feel like to be worth half a million dollars?

It's year 15. You're a GySgt now. You shelve investment #3 and start #4 based on your GySgt income of $4044 per month. 1/3 of this is $1348. You set up the allotment for $1348 and let it ride for 5 years, at the end of which it's grown to $119898.58. Meanwhile investment #1 is now worth $610407.56, investment #2 is now worth $427160.74, and investment #3 is now worth $233338.83. You're retiring from the Marines after 20 years and you now have a nice nest-egg of $1,390,805.71, plus a paltry retirement of about $2000 per month (before taxes)!

At this point, if you leave your investments in place and do nothing else, other than continue to invest like Warren Buffet does, you'll be earning about $265k a year in interest, plus you'll receive another $24k a year in retirement pay (increasing for cost of living) for the rest of your life. Can you live on $289k per year? I sure could.

You could also just get a job to live on, and leave your investments in place. If you let them ride beyond retirement while your start your second career, here's what it'll be worth:

| | |
|---|---|
| 5 years after retirement: | $3,318,954.30 |
| 10 years after retirement: | $7,920,198.73 |
| 20 years after retirement: | $45,103,027.33 |
| 30 years after retirement: | $256,847,478.64 |
| 40 years after retirement: | $1,462,665,173.14 |

**Does an extra $1.4 *billion* dollars make learning a little bit about investing worth doing for you?**

So, that's the secret. 1) You have to invest. You absolutely HAVE to! If you don't, your future is fucked. 2) If you're willing to learn how to invest like the big guys, guys that have PROVEN success, you could make a killing.

For those of you that want to learn more and invest like the big

dogs, you have to read a few books. You don't have to read 300 of

them like I did though. After reading all those books, I realized that 3

of them contained everything I needed to know to invest like the best

investors in history, and I could do so without freaking out about

what the stock market is doing from day to day. In fact, if you learn

what these 3 books teach, you could drop off the face of the earth for

a few years, and still be reasonably sure your investments will

continue to grow.

The books I recommend are:

1) **The Motley Fool You Have More Than You Think :
   The Foolish Guide To Personal Finance**. Publication
   Date: January 2, 2001 | ISBN-10: 0743201744

2) **The Motley Fool Investment Guide: How a Fool
   Beat's Wall Street's Wise Men and How You can
   Too**. Publication Date: January 2, 2001 | ISBN-10:
   0743201736

3) **The New Buffettology: The Proven Techniques for
   Investing Successfully in Changing Markets That
   Have Made Warren Buffett the World's Most**

**Famous Investor.** Publication Date: September 3, 2002

| ISBN-10: 0684871742

About these books:

#1 is a book that should be read by the person that knows absolutely nothing about money. If you can balance your check book, but know little else, this is the book for you. You MUST start with this one to have any hope of understanding the other two.

#2 is a book that should be read by the person that would like to learn about investing. This book is a dry read, meaning that it could be boring for some. Don't let that stop you! FORCE YOUR WAY through this book! It will teach you about investing, about the markets, about funds and stocks. This is definitely a MUST READ, even if you already understand some about investing. This book will be a real bitch to read for many, just try to remember that you will be paying yourself about $1.4 billion over your lifetime for reading it.

#3 is a book for the new investor that just finished book #2. If you skip book #2, you probably won't understand much of this book. This book has all the magic. Once you've read this and understood its principles, you should be able to confidently invest in a company of your choice without worry or fear. You will truly be a value minded investor and have all the tools to realize returns that most others don't. You will be the "contrarian" investor.

That's it for money. I've given you a super-quick outline of your potential earnings if you choose to be an average investor, and your potential earnings if you choose to be above average. You can take advantage of my years of reading by choosing to read only those books that can teach you the skills of value investing in a way that has been proven several times over by some of the greatest investors in history, or, you could do nothing and live in a house on wheels for the rest of your life.

The choice is yours, but **inaction is still a choice** and that choice results in living in a van done by the river (thank you Chris Farley).

## 11 WHAT'S REALLY IMPORTANT

Not everyone will make the Marine Corps a career. There's absolutely nothing wrong with doing your time, then getting out to pursue the rest of your life. Some Marines will decide to re-enlist. After a second tour, only some of those will re-enlist again. Most people I meet consider the 12 year mark to be the point of no return. If you don't get out at 12 years, it usually makes sense to stick it out until the 20 year mark.

If you make the Marine Corps a career, at some point along your career-path you're whole mind-set is going to change. For me it was right around the time I became a father at the age of 30. At some point all the testosterone-stoked vibrato and macho confidence will become a little more reserved. You become that quiet professional that sits in the back of the room, taking everything in and giving input when needed, instead of the typical alpha-male type that does

everything with a ridiculous amount of over-the-top energy.

This is the change. No, not the "change" your grandma is going

through. This is the change that occurs in most career Marine's when

they finally understand what is really important. What is really

important is your Marines. That's it. Yes, we do the missions and the

deployments. We do the planning, training and execution with a

confident professionalism and enthusiasm. But at the end, the

Marines that you lead are the most important thing in the world. I

dare say, more important even than the mission. Without Marines,

our missions don't get accomplished.

Many of us use to debate which is more important, the mission

or troop welfare. Marine Corps leadership dictates that the mission is

the most important thing. After you've completed a few missions,

and eaten shit a few times with other Marines in some god-awful

crap-hole of a country, you'll probably start to see that, even though

we harp on mission accomplishment, mission accomplishment,

mission accomplishment, it's all about the men and women that

stepping forward to serve as cannon fodder for those missions. Is there any more noble a thing in humanity than to give yourself so that others don't have to?

So I said all that to say, the mission is important. It is the focus, but the magic of the Marine Corps is in the individual Marines. Toward the end of my career, I was in awe of some of the things I saw Marines do. Looking back, I'm even in awe of my own willingness to do some of the things I did to get the mission done.

The Marine Corps is an incredible institution and a world-class, robust force in the world. The Marine Corps is the Marines. Without the Marines, there is no Corps.

Therefore, leading Marines is a privilege. It doesn't matter if you're leading one or 200,000 of them. You have the privilege of leading Marines that can each individually adapt, improvise and overcome. If given the commanders intent and enough latitude to adjust, they can make anything happen, even things that are totally outside of their area of expertise. They can find solutions to problems that would cripple or paralyze the average person with fear and indecision.

If you are charged with leading a Marine or a number of Marines, you are responsible to them. You work for them, not the other way around. You see, every Marine, even the Commandant, is given orders from some higher authority. The leader is charged with making those orders happen. He or she develops a plan, issues orders (and commanders' intent) then supervises the action. The Marines make it happen.

The great thing about the Marine is, that if the command or supervisor disappears, there's a very high likelihood that the mission will still be accomplished, because EVERY Marine understands the objective. Every Marine understands the Commanders intent. Therefore, even one lone Marine is capable of changing the outcome of the battle, engagement or task.

This is "Big Picture" stuff I'm relaying to you here. I hope you take the time to read and understand it. Take it to heart, because it's the truest thing you'll ever read about the Marines, and it's important to understand, if you're ever privileged enough to lead Marines.

Lastly, as a leader of Marines you'll be called upon and expected to be totally unselfish and giving to your Marines and to the mission.

I spent the first 10 years of my career giving, and never once did anything to benefit myself personally. Only as I drew closer to retirement did I consider that the Marine Corps would not always be there for me.

For years I worked 6 days a week while other Marines took time off to go to college classes. For years I was the first to work in the morning and the last to leave at night. The higher in rank I got, the more time I spent making sure other Marines had what they needed for their jobs and their families. My focus was always outward on the Marines around me. If you do as I did, you may realize at some point that you let your own interests lapse.

My advice to you is, try to remember to do something for yourself, or your future, at least once a year. If that one thing is starting an investment program like the one I mentioned, that would be a great place to start. College is also a huge thing that will really help you grow and understand the world around you. As I write this, the Marine Corps will pay up to 100% of your tuition for school while you're on active duty. Take advantage of it! Frankly, I think a college degree isn't worth shit. I've known too many people that had them that were complete idiots. However, the education you get from getting the degree is priceless. Of course, an educated idiot is still an idiot, but if you have the education, you at least have the opportunity to reach any goal you set for yourself. The idiots just have to work a lot harder to reach them.

Want to be an astronaut? No problem. Start taking college classes. Within a few short years you'll be eligible for an officer program. Get into it, try really hard to get the highest grades and scores on everything you do, and become a jet pilot (I think only the top of the class in OCS gets selected for fixed-wing flight school). Fly F-18's for a few years; do the "Top Gun" thing, then volunteer for test pilot school. A few years of doing that and you're now a prime candidate to become a space vehicle pilot. Once you're in that position, you may find yourself piloting the first manned trip to Mars.

You can do anything as a Marine. Absolutely anything. You just need someone to show you the way by pointing out the opportunities. In the absence of a good leader that is showing all this stuff to you, look up the MCO 5000.14 (the MCAP) and look up the Marine Corps policy manuals on all these programs yourself. If you can read, you can find a referral to any subject in that manual.

So, bottom line here is that you're going to be really busy. The higher rank you earn, the more busy you'll be. But always, always, at least once a year, do something for yourself, even if you have to take leave to do it. Doing so is the difference between getting out of the Corps as tired shell of a human being or getting out as someone who is raring to go with tons of opportunity in front of them.

## 12 FINISHING UP

In conclusion, I'd like to briefly hit on a few more topics.

Combat is an important thing to Marines. We train for it every day.

Everything we do is geared toward being able to perform in a combat

environment. Every time I've seen Marines presented with an

opportunity to enter a combat zone, they've always been very

enthusiastic and excited to get in there and do their part to make

things happen.

No matter how much we train or how hard we work, there's no

way to know how combat will affect us individually. Everyone is

different and everyone's brain naturally deals with the extremes of

combat in their own unique way. You may be the biggest, toughest

man in your 1500 Marine regiment, but when bullets start flying in

your direction, you may very well crap yourself and end up being totally useless. You just don't really know how you'll react until you're in it. The more you train, rehearse and practice, the less likely you are to suffer any immediate negative effects of combat. But everyone suffers negative effects of some kind, sooner or later.

So, if you get in "the shit" and someone folds up and becomes completely useless, that person has just become a casualty. Some are hit with bullets, some with bombs, and some take an exposure shot to the brain and it totally fucks them up. They aren't cowards or no-loads, they are just a fellow Marine that has become a casualty. Treat them as such and move on with the mission.

The best defense against combat fatigue or Post Traumatic Stress Disorder is training and practice, but no amount of training and practice can guarantee that you won't become a casualty of combat, even after you've returned from the combat zone. So, keep an eye out for your fellow Marines. If they need help, get it for them. If you need help, get it for yourself. There is no shame in getting the help you need. Anybody that says there is should be considered an ignorant douche and ignored. No competent leader would deny a Marine either psychiatric or medical care, unless their unit was in imminent peril... like at risk of being over-run by the enemy.

A little bit about Officers. As a young enlisted man, I really
didn't like Officers. It seemed like they always showed up just in time
to fuck things up or that they had no idea what they were doing
technically, but they still wanted to be the decision maker, and I
couldn't stand that crap. I confess, during this time I was being
exposed to young, inexperienced officers and I myself was young,
arrogant, only slightly more experienced than those officers and
certainly over confident. Technically, I was great at my job, but that
was pretty much the extent of my skill set.

Obviously, this was before I really learned anything about
leadership. If you've read the previous chapter on leadership, you'll
know that leaders aren't perfect. Leaders have to learn to be leaders,
and they usually aren't that great at it when they start out. It is the job
of the senior enlisted Marines to guide the junior Officers in the
absence of a senior Officer guidance. If junior offers don't have that
guidance, they could become a real hazard to productivity.
Sometimes, even with guidance from both senior enlisted and senior
officers, junior officers just don't get it. Marines like this don't last

long, but while you're working for them, it's your job to execute their

intent and do it in a way that make them look as good as possible.

I worked for a Capt like this once. I was a GySgt. My MSgt

NCOIC and I spent a full year and a half trying to keep this guy from

stepping on his own dick, from making counter-productive decisions,

and from leading our platoon into a train wreck of oblivion. The

Capt was a fucking moron that refused to accept any idea that wasn't

his own. We spent hours, weeks and months trying to get this guy to

understand his job and the mission of our small unit, but we never

got through to him. He was ultimately fired and sent to a remote post

for the remainder of his tour. My MSgt was almost fired right

alongside him, but the LtCol in charge recognized the difficulty that

the NCOIC had in getting ANYTHING across to this stubborn

Capt, so he let him stay on.

You will run into leaders like this once in a while. You may have

to live with them for a while, but sooner or later, they'll be gone and

you'll have a more competent and capable officer in his/her place.

Even though that officer was an idiot, even though he probably

couldn't intelligently plan a head call, it was my obligation to try to

help him lead, plan, make decisions and run his platoon. I loyally did that every day of that year and a half. I gave him the respect a Marine

Captain deserves, every day, even when he occasionally attempted to

publicly humiliate me just because he thought he could. I was a

professional, he was a douche, and a douche can only hide for so

long.

This Captains biggest problem was that he refused to truly

consider any other opinion outside of his own, and he was ultimately

fired because of it. Remember I said that leadership is learned, and

some people are slow learners. Your task is trying to help that slow

learner, learn a little faster and shield your Marines from un-necessary

stupidity from above as best as you can.

After Capt Douche was fired, one of our 1stLt's took over the

platoon. He was a very bright guy. He was former enlisted as a

SNCO and was always willing to hear options and opinions from his

staff. Any intelligent person would, wouldn't they?

Anyway, our new Lt's turned out to be pretty good. Even so, we

had one SSgt that ran one crew who refused to speak with him unless

he absolutely had to. SSgt Chuckle-head (not his real name:) thought

that going in to speak to the platoon commander amounted to

"kissing ass". Really? Until that point I thought SSgt Chuckle-head was a reasonably smart person. Think about it. If you come to work every day and the first thing you do is brief your team on what the priorities of work for that day are, don't you think it would be logical to first talk to your boss, to find out what those priorities should be? Don't you think that there could be some special instructions that your OIC needs to pass on to you? Just the possibility that this could happen is reason enough for a SNCO to go speak with the Officer in charge before starting each day.

SSgt Chuckle-head didn't see it that way. To him, speaking with an officer in the officers office was ass-kissing, and by god, he was not going to kiss anyone's ass! Several years later, that same SNCO, now a GySgt, tried pulling the same shit with another OIC we had at a different duty station. This time, he didn't want to follow orders regarding his personal training. This GySgt was great at keeping the moral of his Marines up, and his Marines did their job. But, the Commandant directed that GySgt's within our MOS must do a certain amount of additional training, and this GySgt was more interested in leading his Marines by direction and had little interest in more personal training.

Marines are suppose to "lead by example", not by direction. If you want your Marines to train hard, you better be training hard. Speaking with your OIC daily to get up to speed on operational changes and other new information is not kissing ass or a sign of weakness, it's a sign of intelligence and respect.

Don't let testosterone get in the way of you being a productive and loyal asset to the Marine Corps. Watching this GySgt, whom I considered a personal friend, behave this way was incredibly disappointing, and I hope that at some point he figured out that he didn't have to be that way. Further, he would have better served his Marines had he swallowed his pride and done both aspects of his job.


Last thing I want to say here is that, after reading all this, you should be in a great position to make a career plan for yourself. If that plan is do 4 years and get the hell out, great! Do that. But if you'd like to make it a career, make a plan that will get you to your goal.

If you want to be an astronaut, there are very specific steps you'll need to take to make that happen. If you want to be a SgtMaj, there are very specific step you need to take for that also. Any Marine that is already in the position you want can tell you how they got there. If you want to be an astronaut, first talk to an F-18 pilot and find out how he got there. We don't typically have a lot of astronauts walking around.

The Marine Corps is like a mirror. It will definitely give back to you what you put into it and more. There is no glass ceiling in the Marine Corps. You will only be limited by the knowledge that you have and your willingness to seek out knowledge that you don't have. When it comes to your career, don't ever take someone's word for Marines Corps policy. Always look it up for yourself. It's just too easy to do. Open the MCO 5000.14 and look up the order that pertains to whatever you're trying to learn about. Then download that order and read it. Anyone with a 10th grade education can do it.

The last chapter provides a list of miscellaneous USMC terms and acronyms for your review. I hope you've found this book insightful and not too "preachy". My sincere goal is to help younger Marines understand the Marines Corps a little better and give them the kind of insight I would give a LCpl or NCO as a MSgt. Unfortunately, young enlisted Marines seldom get direct input from a senior enlisted Marines until they are in some sort of trouble. It's a shame to, because I think young Marines, especially those that are seriously considering a career in the Marines, are really thirsty for more experienced and seasoned knowledge available from the senior enlisted ranks. It's just not the same as the guidance you get from a Marine that has like 2 more years in the Corps than you have.

Anyway, hope this book was even a little bit useful. For more information on any subject at all, make an appointment to speak with a senior enlisted Marine of your choice, and ask them for advice. Trust me, they love to talk and will happily talk with you. All you have to do is ask.

## 13 LIST OF USMC ACRONYMS AND TERMS

**0-9**

**29 Stumps** – Marine Corps Air Ground Combat Center Twenty Nine Palms, so named for its location.

**360** – complete circle on a compass (360°); cover all directions around our position.

**72, & 96** – in hours, the standard holiday periods of three, or four days of liberty.

**5.56mm Kiss** - a scar or blister resulting from a burn suffered (usually on the neck) due to hot brass.

**7 Day Store** – on base convenience store.

**782 gear or deuce gear** – standard issue web gear, combat gear, or field equipment, such as ALICE, MOLLE, or ILBE. Named after standard Marine Corps Form 782, which Marines formerly signed when they took custody of and responsibility for their equipment.

**8th & I** – nickname for Marine Barracks, Washington, D.C. so named from its street address at the corner of 8th and I Streets.

**A**

**"A to B"** – when you're in a single file line, it's considered "Asshole to Belly-button".

**Above my/your pay grade** – expression denying responsibility or authority (indicating that the issue should be brought to higher-ranking officials).

**Acquire** – euphemism denoting theft, or horse-trading for needed gear.

**ALICE Pack** – An older version of the back pack previously used by Marines in combat.

**Ahoy** – traditional nautical greeting, used for hailing other boats.[8]

**Air Force Salute** – to say, "I don't know" by a shrug.

**Air Force pockets/Army gloves** – an individual's hands being inside his or her pockets.

**ALICE** – All-purpose Lightweight Individual Carrying Equipment, an older form of combat gear still in occasional use in some Marine activities, replaced by MOLLE and ILBE.

**All Hands** – entire ship's company or unit personnel, including all officers and enlisted personnel; also, the official Navy magazine.

**Alpha's/Class A's** – Service Alpha uniform from the phonetic letter A.

**Amtrac/Amtrack** – amphibious tractor; not to be confused with the railroad company Amtrak.

**ANGLICO** – Air Naval Gunfire Liaison Company.

**Ant farm/Ant hill** – Location with a large number of radio antennae.

**APC** – An armored personnel carrier.

**ASP** – Ammunition Supply Point, where ammo is stored and issued. See also AHA.

**ASVAB waiver** -- a person of below average intelligence or ability; implies that the individual did not get a passing score on the Armed Services Vocational Aptitude Battery or ASVAB for the MOS that they have been assigned.

**Ass pack** – small pack worn around the belt above the buttocks. Same as Fanny Pack or Butt Pack.

**As you were** – order to disregard the immediately preceding order, often in response to a call to "attention on deck" or when the orders issued were mistaken, commonly misused as "as I was".

**Ate up** – person that is totally screwed up; one who is unsatisfactory or .

## Aviation units – See also active squadrons, inactive squadrons, & aviation support units

**H&HS** – Headquarters and Headquarters Squadron, operationally and administratively run USMC Air Stations.
**HAMS** – Headquarters and Maintenance Squadron, also H&MS
**HMX**1 – Marine Presidential Helicopter Squadron
**HMH** – Marine Heavy Helicopter Squadron
**HMLA** – Marine Light Attack Helicopter Squadron
**HMLA/T** – Marine Light Attack Helicopter Training Squadron
**HMM** – Marine Medium Helicopter Squadron
**HMT** – Marine Heavy Helicopter Training Squadron
**HMM/T** – Marine Medium Helicopter Training Squadron
**LAAD Bn** – Low-altitude Air Defense Battalion
**MACG** – Marine Air Command Group
**MACS** – Marine Air Control Squadron
**MAMS** – Marine Aircraft Maintenance Squadron
**MASS** – Marine Air Support Squadron
**MALS** – Marine Aviation Logistics Squadron
**MATCS** – Marine Air Traffic Control Squadron (joined the MACS in the late 1990's)
**MOTS** – Marine Operational Training Squadrons
**MTACS** – Marine Tactical Air Command Squadron
**MWSS** – Marine Wing Support Squadron
**MWCS** – Marine Wing Communications Squadron
**MWHS** – Marine Wing Headquarters squadron
**VMAQ** – Marine Electronic Warfare Squadron
**VMA** – Marine Attack Squadron
**VMAT** – Marine Attack Training Squadron
**VMF** – Marine Fighter Squadron
**VMF/A** – Marine Fighter Attack Squadron
**VMF/A(AW)** – Marine All-Weather Fighter Attack Squadron
**VMFAT** – Marine Fighter Attack Training Squadron
**VMGR** – Marine Aerial Refueler/Transport Squadron
**VMGRT** – Marine Aerial Refueler/Transport Training Squadron
**VMM** – Marine Medium Tiltrotor Squadron
**VMMT** – Marine Medium Tiltrotor Training Squadron

**VMO** – Marine Observation Squadron (De-commissioned in mid 1990's, flew the OV-10)
**VMU** – Unmanned Aerial System Squadron
**VMX** – Marine Tiltrotor Operational Test and Evaluation Squadron

**Aye-aye** or **Aye** – naval term used as a response to orders meaning "I understand the orders and will carry them out".

# B
**Bag nasty**, a bagged or boxed lunch provided by a base chow hall, usually contains a sandwich (ham, turkey, or bologna), fruit, and a small bag of potato chips; often served with a beverage such as juice or milk.
**Back on the block** – behaving informally, like you did before you went to boot camp.
**BAH** – basic Allowance for Housing, a pay supplement that allows a service member to maintain housing appropriate for his or her dependents when not living in government quarters; formerly known as Basic Allowance for Quarters (BAQ).
**BAMCIS** – mnemonic for the troop leading steps, a tactical operation process, stands for: Begin the planning, Arrange reconnaissance, Make reconnaissance, Complete the planning, Issue orders, Supervise the action.
**Barracks cover** – fabric-covered frame cap, worn green with the service uniform and white with the dress uniform.
**Barracks rat** – service member who rarely voluntarily leaves his or her living quarters.[16]
**BAS** – Battalion Aid Station, a unit's medical post ashore for routine illnesses and injuries; **also** Basic Allowance for Subsistence, a pay supplement that allows a service member to feed him or her self while living on the economy (not going to the chow hall for daily mails).
**Battalion Lance Corporal** – most senior non-NCO in the unit; the Lance Corporal who, while having a lot of time in grade, is the least likely to be promoted to the rank of Corporal, most like because of something in his or her record preventing promotion. See also terminal lance
**Battery operated grunt** – a field radio operator.

**Battle buddy** – sarcastic euphemism deriving from orders for Marines to not go on liberty alone when stationed overseas, also an actual Army term in which soldiers are taught to stay together in a combat zone.

**Battle zero, battle sight zero or BZO** – calibrated settings on the sights of a weapon that allow the shooter to overcome various factors and hit accurately at a given range, used as a default sight setting before adjusting windage or elevation; also used as a verb when firing to triangulate a BZO by firing a group at a known range, then adjusting the front sight post to hit center mast.

**BB counter or BB stacker** – service member whose duties relate to the storage, issue, or handling of ordnance.

**BCGs or BCs** – Birth Control Glasses or Boot Camp Glasses, unattractive standard military issue glasses worn at recruit training and beyond; so named because the wearer presumably has difficulty influencing the opposite sex into sexual relations.

**Beans, bullets and bandages** – expression used to refer to logistics planning for the unit: rations, ammunition, and medical care.

**Beer garden** – area set aside for the social consumption of alcohol and smoking of tobacco; Usually located close to living quarters and may contain barbecue or picnic facilities.

**Beer-thirty** – time of dismissal from the day's duties. See also COB.

**Belay** – to cancel an order; to stop; to firmly secure a line.

**Below** – down the ladder well; a lower floor, or below decks.

**Bent Dick** – a directionally broken nose gun on an AH-1 Cobra.

**BEQ** – Bachelor Enlisted Quarters, living spaces for single enlisted Marine, usually a barracks.

**BCD** – Bad Conduct Discharge, also nicknamed **Big Chicken Dinner**.

**Big green weenie** – an expression denoting that a Marine has been screwed or "hooked up" in an undesirable way by the Marine Corps, usually in relation to an inconvenience or unpleasant duty.

**Billet** – specific role or job within the unit (for example, the billet of Company First Sergeant is held by a senior enlisted advisor, usually a First Sergeant, but could be a Master Sergeant or Gunnery Sergeant). Billets are a job, not a rank.

**Bird** – term used to describe communications satellites used by the military for Satellite Communications (SATCOM); also sometimes used as a generic term for aircraft.

**Blanket party** – group assault on a service member, repeatedly striking him or her, preceded by covering the victim's head by a blanket so he or she cannot identify the perpetrators. This is a crime and should not be engaged in… there are other ways to fix people.

**Blood stripe** – scarlet trouser stripe worn on the blue dress trousers, awarded to Marine officers and NCOs due to their high fatality rates in the Battle of Chapultepec. Also a form of hazing where fellow NCO's inflict damage to the outer thighs of a newly promoted Corporal, also a serious violation of the UCMJ.

**Blouse** – military dress coat, jacket or shirt; or as a verb to tuck one's trousers into boot-bands or otherwise secure pant legging.

**BLT** – Battalion Landing Team, the ground combat element of a MEU; not a Bacon, Lettuce, and Tomato sandwich.

**Blues** – Blue Dress uniform.

**Bn** – abbreviation for battalion.

**Boat** – any naval vessel, considered a derogatory term because all commissioned vessels other than submarines are known as "ships".

**Body Armor** – Bullet and shrapnel proof clothing, usually for torso, groin and neck.

**Boondoggle** – wasteful project or trip on government time and/or expense that serves no purpose other than to entertain the person making it.

**Boot** – recruit, or demeaning term for a Marine just out of training.

**Boots and utes** or **boots'n'utes** – boots and utility uniform, minus the blouse and cover; sometimes used for physical training, Martial Arts Training or working in hot environments.

**Boot bands or boot blousers** – elastic straps or coiled springs used to roll trouser legging under at the top of the boot and simulate tucking into the boot itself; used in blousing boots.

**Boot camp** – recruit training for enlisted Marines at Parris Island, SC and San Diego, CA.

**BOQ** – Bachelor Officer Quarters, housing for single Marine officers.

**Box-kicker** – demeaning term for service member who works in supply, specifically, a warehouse clerk.

**Brain bucket** – helmet.

**Brain-housing group** – your head. Sometimes referring to the mind and it's sharpness.

**Brass** – expended round casings from weapons; brass uniform items; term for senior officers due to the metal of their rank insignia.

**Brat** – longtime dependent children.

**Brig** – prison or place of confinement aboard ship or ashore at a Marine Corps or naval station.

**Brig rat** – person who has served much brig time, a habitual offender.

**Brightwork** – brass or shiny metal.

**Broke-dick(s)** – service member on light, limited, or no duty status for medical reasons; also slang for the old-school dress shoes that you have to polish.

**Brown-bagger** – a service member (usually married) who lives off base with his family, termed because he or she receives an allowance to buy their food instead of eating every meal at the chow hall.

**Buddy-fucker** – negligent or malicious disregard for another service member's career, welfare, or comfort, often for personal gain.

**Bug juice** – insect repellent; also, a colorful, fruity-tasting beverage made from a dry mix (such as Kool-Aid).

**Bulkhead** – Naval term for a wall.

**Bum scoop** – bad information.

**Bus driver** – Air Force pilot; also someone who habitually says things that get other people in trouble.

**Busted or busted down** – reduced in rank.

**Butt pack** – small waist pack worn around the belt above the buttocks, similar to Fanny Pack.

**Butts** – pit(s) on a shooting range where targets are located, pulled and services. See also pits and pull butts.

**Butter bar** – 2nd Lieutenant, so named for the single gold bar rank insignia.

**By the numbers** or **Barney-style** – to perform an action in sequence and strictly according to instructions, idiot proof, oversimplified for the benefit of people that don't catch on quickly..

**By your leave** – expression used to render respect when overtaking a senior Marine or Sailor that is walking in the same direction (in conjunction with a salute); traditionally, the senior must offer permission before the junior passes him or her.

# C

**CACO** – Casualty Assistance Calls/Counseling Officer, a Marine detailed to help the family of a Marine killed, wounded, or captured in the line of duty.

**California Marine** – Marine currently or formerly stationed in California; typically tends to walk across grass, directly to destinations, where east coast and Okinawa Marines tend to use the sidewalks and roads.

**Cammies** – camouflage utility uniform.

**Campaign cover** – official term for the brown campaign hat worn by drill instructors.

**Cannon cocker** – artilleryman.

**Captain's mast** – office hours afloat. The term "Captain's Mast" is almost universally negative, implying non-judicial punishment.

**Carrier landings** – When a fixed-wing aircraft lands on an aircraft carrier; also, when a long, sturdy table is cleared, hosed down with alcohol, and Marines run and dive onto the table (usually in a dress uniform) sliding down the table and hopefully stopping before coming to the end. This is usually only done during a major celebration, like a mess night or Marine Corps Ball.

**Carry on** – order to continue after being interrupted.

**CAS** – Close Air Support, aircraft fire on enemy ground troops in support of nearby friendly troops.

**CAS-EVAC** – CASualty EVACuation, emergency evacuation of injured personnel from combat zone by any modes of transport available, as opposed to a MEDEVAC carried out by ambulance equipment designed solely for the purpose.

**Casual Company** – a holding unit for Marines awaiting one of the following: discharge from the Corps, training (usually at a formal school), or deployment to a unit.

**CAX** – combined arms exercise.

**CBRN** – Chemical, Biological, Radiological, and Nuclear. See also NBC.

**CCU** – Correctional Custody Unit, a hard-labor and heavy discipline unit overseen by MPs or Navy Masters-at-Arms to which Marines and Sailors found guilty of minor UCMJ offenses through NJP are sent for up to 30 days in lieu of confinement in the brig.

**CFT** – Combat Fitness Test; similar to a PFT but focuses on combat strength and endurance.

**Chair Force** – derogatory term for the US Air Force. see
**Chair-borne** or **chair-borne ranger** – someone who works in an
office environment.
**Charlies** or **chucks** – The service "C" uniform, consisting of the
short-sleeve khaki shirt and green trousers.
**Chaser** – an escort for one or more prisoners.
**Check fire** – order to stop firing due to a safety condition, possible
error or mis-target.
**Chesty** – First name of a historically significant and highly decorated
Marine Officer used in reference to Marines that have been awarded
many ribbons and medals.
**Chevron** – symbols of enlisted ranks above private.
**Chit** – voucher, receipt, letter, or note, entitling the bearer to special
treatment, such as medical restrictions from duty.
**CIF** – Consolidated Issue Facility, a place on a base where all
organizational personal combat equipment is stored and issued.
**CID** - Criminal Investigation Division, Federal law enforcement
agency of the U.S. Marine Corps whose mission it is to conduct
official criminal investigations into misdemeanor and felony offenses
committed on Marine Corps installations as may directed and not
under the primary jurisdiction of the Naval Criminal Investigative
Service (NCIS).
**Cinderella liberty** – liberty expiring at midnight.
**Civ div** – civilian division, term used to describe civilian life after
getting out of the Marines.
**Civvies** – civilian clothing or mufti.
**CLP** – Cleaner, Lubricant, Preservative, teflon-based cleaning and
lubricating fluid used for maintaining small arms. Also slang for
coffee.
**Cluster-fuck** – chaotic and messy situation, usually the result of
multiple mistakes or problems happening in rapid succession. See
also goat rope / goat fuck.
**CMC** – acronym for Commandant of the Marine Corps.
**COB** – Close Of Business, the end of working hours; or Close Order
Battle, a synonym for Close Quarters Battle.
**COC** - Combat Operations Center, the command post for a combat
arms unit, usually of battalion-size or larger.
**CONUS** – CONtinental United States (48 states excluding Alaska
and Hawaii), as opposed to OCONUS.

**Corframs** – uniform dress shoes made from imitation leather, very shiny and preferred to Broke-Dicks.

**Corpsman** – Navy hospital corpsman attached to a Marine unit; also known as "doc".

**Cover** – a hat or helmet; also protection from enemy fire.

**Cover and alignment** – when in a formation, this refers to the proper distance between those next to, in front of, and behind a person; to seek the proper interval. Don't think too hard about this, it'll become second nature in boot camp.

**Covered** – when wearing a hat, you're covered; or when protected from direct enemy fire by something bullet-proof, like a big rock.

**Cover Block** – an (usually metal) insert meant to fit inside of and stretch the cover of your utility uniform. Very popular from the 1980's to 2000 or so, not so much now that covers are stitched.

**CQB or CQC** – Close Quarters Battle/Combat, combat within a confined space, such as a house; urban warfare.

**Crew-served weapon** - also larger fire arm, that requires 2 or more Marines to fully operate.

**Cruise** – Navy term for deployment aboard ship; also called a Float.

**CS** – tear gas or 2-chlorobenzalmalononitrile, a white solid powder commonly used for CBRN defense training.


# D
**Daily 7 or daily 16** – stretches and exercises used as a warm-up for other, more strenuous physical training.

**Deck** – floor or surface of the earth; to punch or knock down with one blow.[35]

**Deep six** – to dispose of by throwing overboard ship.

**Detachment (Det)** – a portion of a unit sent independently of its parent organization, usually in support of a larger headquarters; or a small standalone unit isolated geographically from its parent command.

**Deuce** – reference to the number two in various unit or equipment names; the senior intelligence officer for a unit.

**Deuce gear** – see 782 gear, from the last digit in that term.

**Devil Dog** – term of endearment amongst Marines; see also Leather-Neck.

**Devil dogged** – Being corrected by another Marine for some minor deficiency, often in public; this term was created by young Marines that noticed senior enlisted usually only use the term "Devil Dog" when they're about to correct a junior Marine in public.

**Devil pup** – nickname for a Marine's child(ren); a member of the Young Marines; a patronizing nickname for a junior Marine.

**DI** – Drill Instructor.

**DI hut or duty hut** – office for drill instructors in a platoon's squad bay; doubles as sleeping quarters for the drill instructor on duty.

**Dick-skinner** or **dick-beater** – your own hand.

**Diddy bop** – walking or marching in a manner that does not present a crisp military appearance.

**Diet Private** – A recruit in Boot Camp who has been deemed overweight according to USMC Standards. These recruits are usually the last through the chow line and have their meal content closely inspected by DI's.

**Doc or Devil Doc** – Navy hospital corpsman attached to the Marines; Devil Doc is a term of respect normally reserved for Corpsmen who are Fleet Marine Force qualified or who have served in combat with Marines.

**Dog** – small metal fitting used to secure watertight doors, hatches, covers, scuttles, etc.; also, to close/secure such door/hatch; also, slang for Marine, from the term Devil Dog.

**Dog and pony show** – any display, demonstration, or appearance by Marines at the request of seniors for the pleasure of someone else (usually civilians, congresspersons or foreign military), such as a ceremony, parade or capability demonstration; also, a derogatory term for the usual requirement to over-perfect such a performance.

**Doggie** – enlisted member of the United States Army, from the diminutive "dog-face".

**Donkey dick** – slang for virtually any piece of equipment which has a generally cylindrical or phallic shape with unknown, or obscure nomenclature.

**Dope** – information, or sight settings and/or wind corrections for a rifle under given conditions.

**Downrange or down-range** – dangerous area, the portion of a shooting range that receives impacts.

**DPICM** – Dual-Purpose Improved Conventional Munitions, a specialized artillery round that releases sub-munitions.

**Drill** – close order drill, the procedures and methodology of handling weapons and moving troops from one place to another in an orderly fashion, used to indoctrinate recruits in obedience to commands and military appearance.

**DRMO'd** – to dispose of an item by taking it to the Defense Reutilization and Marketing Office (DRMO).

**Drug deal** - to obtain needed supplies, equipment or services outside of official channels via barter rather than theft.

**Drop a dime** – to reveal incriminating information about a person.

**Dry fire** – practice firing of a weapon without using ammunition in order to refine the shooting fundamentals.

**DTG** – Date, Time Group, a numeric code denoting the time and date, usually of a message.

**Dummy cord** – lanyard or tether used to secure a piece of equipment to an anchor to prevent losing it.

**Duty NCO or duty** – sentry responsible for patrol and security of a specific area (usually a barracks and/or working space in garrison). See also fire watch.

**E**

**EAS** – End of Active Service, the date of discharge from active duty.

**EGA** – Eagle, Globe, and Anchor, the emblem of the Marine Corps, (using this acronym in place of the words Eagle, Globe, and Anchor is frowned upon by some.

**Embed** – often during operations, external assets or journalist are embedded within a combat unit.

**Ensign** – colors, national flag; also the most junior commissioned officer rank in the US Navy.

**EOD** – Explosive Ordnance Disposal, the military version of a bomb squad.

**EPD** – Extra Punitive Duties, punishment assigned where the individual is required to perform cleaning duties after working hours (on his or her liberty time).

**EPW** – Enemy Prisoner of War.

**F**

**Fallen Angel** – Marine Officer who failed to qualify in flight school and is now in another MOS.

**FAP** – Fleet Assistance Program, a program designed to assign fleet Marines to base/station duties while in garrison.

**FARP** – Forward Arming/Refueling Point; a space on the battlefield designated for the re-arming and re-fueling of aircraft, typically close to the focal point of the action. Allows CAS aircraft to quickly re-arm and re-fuel without flying all the way back to a base or ship.

**Fart sack** – linen envelope that is place around a mattress.

**Fat-body** – overweight recruit or service member; AKA: food blister.

**FEBA** – Forward Edge of the Battle Area, the line of departure where a unit enters enemy territory.

**Field day** – day or portion of day set aside for top-to-bottom cleaning of an area; also as a verb for the act of conducting a field day.

**Field expeditionary** – improvisation, to make do with the materials you have on hand.

**Field meet** – organized sporting competition, often involving athletics and/or soldierly skills.

**Field-strip** – to disassemble a piece of ordnance or weapon to the major part groups for routine cleaning or lubricating; also, to strip cigarette butts to their filters before throwing away; also, to remove packaging from major MRE items, then packing it all back into the MRE exterior bag in order to save space.

**Fifty-cal** – M2 Browning machine gun, from its .50 caliber ammunition. See also Ma Deuce.

**Fighting hole** – a defensive position dug into the ground; can be dug for one Marine, a pair, or a weapon crew; formerly known as a "foxhole" or fighting position.

**Final Duty Station** - A reference to a Marine's final posting.

**FPF** -- Final Protective Fire, last ditch effort to repel an attacking enemy. No ammunition is spared.

**FPL** -- Final Protective Line is the inner perimeter around a friendly position, emeny troops approaching the FPL initiates the commencement of final protective fire.

**Fire for effect** – indicates that the adjustment/ranging of indirect fire is satisfactory and the actual effecting rounds should be fired; also a euphemism for telling someone to execute a plan.

**Fire watch** – sentry on duty specifically guarding a person, place, object, or area in a non-combat area (such as a barracks); considered under arms but usually unarmed. See also duty.

**Fire watch medal** – a derogative term for National Defense Service Medal, so named because even recruits earn it despite fire watch being their most difficult duty.

**First shirt** – a company or battery First Sergeant.

**Fitness report** or **Fitrep** – a report written on Marines (sergeant and above) detailing proficiency, conduct and fitness for duty, heavily weighted for promotion.

**Five-jump chump** – a service member who has only performed the minimum five paratrooper jumps to receive the Basic Parachute Insignia, as opposed to the Navy and Marine Corps Parachutist Insignia, which requires additional jumps.

**Flak jacket** – antiquated ballistic vest or body armor.

**Float** – deployment aboard ship.

**FMF** or **fleet** – Fleet Marine Force, the operational forces of the Corps, as opposed to reserve or supporting establishment units (Marine Corps Base or Air Stations).

**FMTU** – Foreign Military Training Unit.

**FNG** – Fucking New Guy.

**FOB** – Forward Operating Base.

**Form ID-10T** or **ID-ten-tango** – prank and fool's errand where an unsuspecting Marine is asked to find the ID-10T form, not knowing it is an orthograph for "idiot". Other similar stupid pranks include: Finding some BA-1100N (fake battery, spells Balloon), finding a bottle of Prop Wash (Prop wash is air turbulence from a running aircraft propeller), finding a spool of Flight Line (Flight Line is the part of an airport on which aircraft park), finding a box of "grid squares" (impossible to do, grid squares are reference lines on a map), registering an arty round (this is when artillery Marines have a new guy run a very heavy artillery round out into a field or around a camp to get it "registered" (registered really mean report and impact of an arty round). All of these are considered hazing and doing these things to new Marines is usually punished severely by Commanders.

**Fortitudine** – former motto of the Corps in the 19th century (replaced by Semper Fidelis), from the Latin word for "fortitude"; also the name of the Marine Corps History Division's quarterly magazine.

**Four Fingers of Death** - nickname for the old frankfurter MRE. I got to sample one of these in S. Korea in 1991 (it had an expiration date of April 1986).

**Foxhole** – fighting hole as termed by the Army and Marines of the past, no longer appropriate for Marine use.

**FRAGO** – FRAGmentary Order, an addendum to a published operational order.

**FragO** – Frag Officer, the guy designated to schedule flight support for major units.

**Frock** – to be authorized to wear the next higher rank before your actual promotion, confers rank authority but not pay grade.

**FUBAR** – Fucked/Fouled Up Beyond All Recognition/Repair. See also SNAFU.

**Full-bird** – Colonel, as opposed to a light-colonel or Lieutenant Colonel; so named because his or her rank insignia is a silver eagle.

**G**

**G-2** – an individual's intellect, from the designation for a staff intelligence organization.

**Gaff off** – to disregard or ignore a person or order, context usually denotes insubordination; to screw around instead of doing work.

**Gaggle-fuck** – group of Marines grouped too closely or in an unorganized fashion; from gaggle, the term for a flock of grounded geese, and cluster fuck, a term for a messy situation.

**Gangway** – ship's passageway; also used to order others to give-way to seniors in passageways, and particularly when going up and down ladders.

**Garrison** – in addition to the traditional meaning, an adjective referring to not being deployed or deployable, such as buildings at a unit's home base.

**Garrison cover** – a rigid circular hat worn with the service uniform.

**Gear** – equipment; usually referring to an individual's combat equipment.

**Gear adrift** – gear found left lying around, unsecured and unguarded.

**Geedunk** – candy and other assorted fat-pills, or a location where such fat pills are obtained (such as a store, vending machine, soda mess or roach-coach).

**General** – method of addressing a Brigadier General, Major General, Lieutenant General, or General.

**General orders** – list of General Orders for Sentries detailing rules for guard or sentry duty.

**GI shower** – forcibly bathing an individual who refuses to bath themselves.

**GITMO** – U.S. Naval Base, Guantanamo Bay, Cuba.

**Glow belt** -- a high visibility belt, used during PT or other night activity.

**Go-fasters** – running shoes or sneakers.

**Goat rope** or **Goat fuck** – chaotic and messy situation. See also cluster fuck.

**Good cookie** – Good Conduct Medal.

**Good to go** – expression denoting that you are ready to go; prepared or satisfactory.

**Gore-Tex** – All Purpose Environmental Clothing System (APECS), a cold/wet weather protective parka, trousers and sleeping bag cover; based on the Extended Cold Weather Clothing System, usually in reference to the parka; from the fabric it is made from.

**Gouge** – information or news. (This book is Great Gouge for a 1$^{st}$ term Marine!)

**Grab-ass** – horseplay, unorganized or screwing around.

**Grid squares** – marked reference lines on a map, typically in kilometers or "klicks".

**Grinder** – parade ground or deck used primarily for drill and formations.

**Ground guide** – person who walks in front of a vehicle in order to detect and avoid obstacles and guide the driver to the proper spot without colliding with anything.

**Grunt** or **ground pounder** – infantryman.

**GT score** – general intelligence measurement, from the General Technical score on the Armed Services Vocational Aptitude Battery (ASVAB); each MOS has a minimum GT score that a Marine must have to qualify for that MOS.

**Guide** – unit guidon-bearer; in recruit training.

**Guidon** – unit flag on a stick top with a pike.

**Gun club** - slang term for the USMC at-large.

**Gung ho** – Chinese phrase meaning to "work together," it became the battle cry of the Marine Raiders.

**Gunner** – shortened form of Marine Gunner, a nickname for an Infantry Weapons Officer; used incorrectly to refer to the Officer In Charge when he or she is of warrant officer rank.

**Gunny** – nickname for Gunnery Sergeant, **NOT** a Master Gunnery Sergeant.

**Gunny rolls** – loosely rolled cammie sleeves, so named from the tendency for some older Marines that tend to do this, as opposed to the LCpl roll, which is extremely tight and rolled up to the shoulder.

**Gyrene** – a stupid nickname for Marine, often thought an insult; combination of the words "GI" and "Marine". Whomever made this one up was a dumb-ass.

# H

**Hajji** – a racist term for Arab or Middle Eastern person or object, from the Arabic term for one who has completed a pilgrimage to Mecca, or "hajj"

**Half-mast** – position of a flag when hoisted half-way up a flag pole (technically 1 or 2 flag-lengths below the top, I think), usually done in respect to a deceased person; also called "half-staff" amongst non-naval forces.

**Hard charger** – term of endearment from a senior to a junior Marine when he or she completes a difficult task, so named for charging through the assignment; or general toughness.

**Hashmark** – service stripe worn on the uniform sleeve by enlisted men and women for completion of four years of honorable service in any of the U.S. Armed Services and Reserves.

**Hat** – nickname for drill instructor, so named for the distinctive campaign cover they wear; usually reserved for other or former drill instructor use.

**Hatch** – Naval term for door; more specifically, the watertight cover over an opening between compartments or that leads to the ladder wells between decks of a ship.

**HDR** – Humanitarian Daily Ration, a variation of the MRE used to feed a single malnourished person for one day with 2,300 calories.

**HE** – High Explosive, used to describe various kinds of ordnance.

**Head** – a nautical term bathroom.

**Head shed** – command post or other headquarters location where senior Marines gather or work.

**Headgear** – covers, helmets, caps, etc.

**HEAT** – High-Explosive Anti-Tank, type of tank round.

**Heavy hat** – junior drill instructor who performs more discipline or punishment tasks than his peers. Often called "the heavy".

**Hell hole** – hatch mounted in the deck of many helicopters (such as the H-53 and the H-46) for rappelling, fast roping and cargo lifting.

**Helo** – Helicopter; "Chopper" is an Army/civilian term.

**HEDP** – High-Explosive Dual Purpose, type of armor piercing ammunition.

**High and to the right** – losing one's temper or rationality; from a common error of a shooter that jerks the trigger and impacts the upper right side of a target.

**High and tight** – nickname for a very high regulation hair cut.

**High-speed** – new, interesting, high tech; sometimes paired with the term "low drag".

**HIMARS** – High Mobility Artillery Rocket System.

**HMFIC** – acronym that NCOIC's like to through around meaning Head Mother-Fucker In Charge.

**HMMWV** or **humvee** – High-Mobility Multi-purpose Wheeled Vehicle, common utility truck.

**Hollywood Marine** – Marine that graduated from Marine Corps Recruit Depot San Diego, stemming from the smack-talking rivalry between the two recruit depots.

**Home-steading** – remaining at one duty station for an extended tour or consecutive tours; usually frowned upon by HQMC monitors.

**Honcho** or **head honcho** – person in charge, from the Japanese word for "boss', "hanchō"; also a nickname for Okinawan taxi drivers.

**hooch** or **hootch** – tent, hut, shelter or other temporary dwelling.

**House mouse** – recruit tasked with cleaning and performing domestic chores in drill instructor-only areas.

**HQMC** – Headquarters Marine Corps.

**Hump** – a forced march carrying full equipment loads; also to carry or lift a load.

**Hurry up and wait** – expression denoting poor time management or planning, often occurs when a senior rushes a unit into a situation early in order to ensure they are "on time".

# I

**I & I** – Inspector and Instructor staff, an active duty Marine assignment to supervise the training and operation of a reserve unit.

**IAW** – In Accordance With, term often used to denote compliance with published orders or procedures.

**IED** – Improvised Explosive Device, bomb constructed, set, and detonated in unconventional warfare; the acronym can be modified to denote a specific type of IED (such as VBIED, a Vehicle Borne IED).

**IG** – Inspector General.

**IG Inspection** – official inspection of a unit by a commanding general or his representatives.

**ILBE** – Improved Load Bearing Equipment, a newer version of personal combat gear, utilizes the PALS, replaced MOLLE.

**In country** – phrase referring to being within a war zone or in a subject country.

**Incentive/individual training or IT** – physical training used as a punishment in recruit training, sometimes nicknamed "getting bent," getting "thrashed", getting "pitted" or "getting destroyed". **Ink stick** – a pen.

**Irish pennant** or **IP** – loose thread or string on a uniform or equipment that detracts from a perfect appearance.

**Iron Mike** – originally a nautical term for a gyrocompass; name for various memorial statues, such as at Parris Island, SC, Quantico, VA, and Belleau, France; nickname bestowed on Marines who score a perfect 300 points on the Physical Fitness Test; nickname for a company or battery named "M or "Mike" in NATO phonetic alphabet.

**IRR** – Individual Ready Reserve, branch of the reserve that most former service members fall under upon the end of active service, may be called to involuntarily return to active status. Enlisted Marines that EAS usually remain in this status until 8 years after their original enlistment date. Retired Marines remain in this status until 30 years after their original enlistment date.

# J

**JAG** – Judge Advocate General, colloquial name for the legal entity within the Marine Corps, more properly called Judge Advocate Division, from the Judge Advocate General of the Navy, the naval officer who oversees both the Navy's and Marine Corps' legal entities.

**Jarhead** – derogatory term for a Marine. Jarhead has several supposed origins: the regulation "High and Tight" haircut resembles a mason jar (to add insult, some note that the jar is an empty vessel).

**Jesus shoes** – government-issue sandals or flip-flops for sanitation in showers. See also shower shoes.

**JJ DID TIE BUCKLE** – mnemonic for the 14 leadership traits: Justice, Judgment, Dependability, Initiative, Decisiveness, Tact, Integrity, Enthusiasm, Bearing, Unselfishness, Courage, Knowledge, Loyalty, Endurance.

**JOB** - Junk On the Bunk, a formal inspection of personal and organizational gear that takes place in the barracks, where the gear is placed on the rack in a pre-designated order.

**Joker** – junior enlisted service member that likes to be a smart-ass.

**JTF** – Joint Task Force, a provisional unit or formation from more than one branch of service.

# K

**K or klicks** – kilometer(s).

**KA-BAR** – fighting/utility knife first issued during World War II. Still in service as of 2012.

**Keeper** – cloth belt loop on the green service blouse to hold the cloth belt neatly in place.

**Kevlar** – helmet made from kevlar.

# L

**Ladder well** – stairway or ladder connecting different decks of a ship.

**Laminated** – perceived semi-permanent state of issue for a normally temporary status, as in "Laminated Light Duty Chit"..

**Lance Colonel** – slang for Lance Corporal denoting a junior Marine with extended time in service or grade.

**Lance Coolie, Lance Criminal** – more slang terms for Lance Corporal.

**Lance Corporal Underground** or **Lance Corporal Network** – a reference to information shared among Lance Corporals working in different parts of a unit; sometimes refers to the spread of foolish rumors that a more experienced Marine might recognize as false.

**Land of the big PX** – used in reference to CONUS by Marines deployed overseas.

**Lawn dart** or **North Carolina Lawn Dart** – derogatory term for an AV-8 Harrier, due to its early tendency to crash when it's single engine failed.

**LBV** – Load Bearing Vest, personal equipment used to keep the most commonly used items within easy reach utilizing the PALS, usually a component of MOLLE or ILBE.

**LCPLIC** – Lance Corporal in Charge. Humorously refers to a salty LCpl.

**Lead stick** – pencil.

**Leatherneck** – nickname for Marine, so named for the stiff leather collars were once worn to protect the throat from sword-blows. The dress blue uniform still bears a high stock collar today.

**Liberty** – authorized free time ashore or off station, not counted as leave. Usually after daily working hours.

**Liberty risk** – a Marine that has a high risk of getting into trouble on liberty.

**Lifer** – career service member, as opposed to one who serves for a single enlistment.

**Lima Charlie or Lickin' Chicken** – Loud and Clear, an expression meaning that a communication has been received and understood; radio phraseology.

**Line company** – lettered Marine companies or the aviation term for ground units, originally, an infantry company.

**Lollygag** – dawdle or fooling around.

**Long War** – term for the War on Terrorism favored by senior military leaders.

**LT** – abbreviation for lieutenant, inappropriate to address as such verbally.

**LWH** – LightWeight Helmet.

**LZ** – Landing Zone, a clearing designated as the place where a helicopter (or other VTOL aircraft) can land.

# M

**M** – a prefix to the model number of a specific nomenclature of equipment, generally considered to denote "model" or "mark".

**Ma'am** – proper method of addressing female officers in particular and all women in general.

Maggie's drawers – red flag attached to a pole, used to signal a miss on the rifle range, replaced by a red disk; also known as "Disked a miss".

**MAGTF** – Marine Air-Ground Task Force.

**Mama-san** – term of endearment for an elder Japanese woman, often a maid, cook, or tailor/seamstress performing services for Marines; from the Japanese honorific suffix "san".

**MARINE** – Muscles Are Required, Intelligence Non-Essential or My Ass Rides In Navy Equipment, acronyms used by other branches.

**Marine** – the following nicknames are usually acceptable: leatherneck, devil dog, sea soldier, warrior, hard charger, motivator; the following are acceptable from other Marines only: jarhead, gyrene; the following are insults: soldier, shit-bird.

**Marine house** – Security Guard term for living quarters for Marines, on or off embassy grounds.

**Master Guns or Master Gunny** – Master Gunnery Sergeant.

**MBT** – Main Battle Tank, currently the M1 Abrams.

**MCI** – Marine Corps Institute, a distance education unit; also, the courses they produce that are available to Marines.

**MCCS** – Marine Corps Community Services (also known by the humorous acronym Marine Corps Crime Syndicate)

**MCCUU** – Marine Corps Combat Utility Uniform.

**MCMAP** – Marine Corps Martial Arts Program.

**MCT** – Marine Combat Training, infantry skills training for non-infantry Marines.

**MCX** – Marine Corps eXchange, a military department store, less formally known as the PX.

**Meat gazer** – urinalysis observer who observes the service member peeing into the sample containers to the legitimacy of the sample.

**MEB** – Marine Expeditionary Brigade.

**MEDEVAC or Medivac** – MEDical EVACuation, removing a wounded person to the closest medical or triage facility using designated ambulance equipment, vehicles, or aircraft.

**MEF** – Marine Expeditionary Force.

**MEPS** – Military Entrance Processing Station, facility where prospective recruits are screened medically, psychologically, and legally for recruit training.

**Mess hall** – cafeteria/chow hall.

**Messman** – cook, or Marine on mess duty that works for the cooks.

**MEU** – Marine Expeditionary Unit.

**Mickey Mouse boots** – boots designed for extreme cold weather using an air bladder for insulation, named for their oversized, bloated appearance.

**Midrats** – midnight (or other late-night) rations provided for service members who work night shifts.

**"Mike"** – used to abbreviate "minute".

**"Mike-mike"** – used to abbreviate "millimeters".

**Military left** - pertaining to the left side of something or the direction to the left of the subject in question. Used sarcastically when someone turns right instead of left.

**Military time** – the time of day on a 24-hour clock. We don't say the word "hours" after each indication of time (that's Army). 0900 would be "Zero nine hundred", not "Oh nine hundred".

**MOLLE** – MOdular Lightweight Load-carrying Equipment, type of load-bearing equipment utilizing the PALS, replaced ALICE and replaced by ILBE.

**Moonbeam** – a flashlight.

**MOPP** – Mission Oriented Protective Posture, the defense equipment (gas masks and over-garment suits) worn to protect against Nuclear, Biological, and Chemical weapons.

**Mosquito wings** – rank insignia for a Private First Class, a single chevron.

**Motivator** – term of endearment from a senior to a junior Marine, so named when the junior displays a motivated attitude.

**Moto** – motivated/motivating, often used to describe motivation in general.

**Motor t or MT** – Motor Transport, a subunit of Marines responsible for the operation and maintenance of wheeled non-combat and non-engineer vehicles.

**MOUT** – Military Operation in Urban Terrain. See also CQB/CQC.

**MOS** – Military Occupational Specialty, a job classification.

**MP** – Military Police..

**MRE** – Meal, Ready-to-Eat, standard U.S. field ration. Sometimes jokingly referred to as "Meals Rejected by the Enemy," "Meals Rejected by Ethiopia," "Meals Rarely Eaten," "Meal, Reluctant to Exit," or "Three Lies for the Price of One".

**MRE bomb** – bursting plastic bag made from chemical heating pouches found inside of a standard MRE.

**MSG** – Marine Corps Security Guard, responsible for guarding United States Embassies.

**MTO** – Motor Transport Officer, the Marine in charge of maintenance and operation of a unit's trucks.

**MTV** – Modular Tactical Vest, the newest type of ballistic vest for Marines, as of 2012.

**MTVR** – Medium Tactical Vehicle Replacement. A 7-ton.

**MWD** – Military Working Dog, a trained government canine for law enforcement, detection of explosives and/or drugs, sentry duty, or other military use(s).


# N

**NBC** – Nuclear, Biological, Chemical. See also CBRN.

**NCIS** – Naval Criminal Investigative Service, the primary law enforcement agency of the Department of the Navy.

**NCO** – Non-Commissioned Officer: corporal or sergeant.

**NCOIC** – Non-Commissioned Officer In Charge, an NCO responsible for a group of Marines, but without the authority of a commissioned officer; See also SNCOIC.

**NJP** – Non-Judicial Punishment, a legal proceeding much like a court-martial of much smaller scope. A commanding officer is authorized to award summary punishments at office hours (called Captain's Mast afloat) under Article 15, UCMJ, to punish offenses too serious to be dealt with by counseling or rebuke, but not serious enough to warrant court-martial.

**NMCI** – Navy/Marine Corps Intranet, the program that outsources garrison information technology services for the Department of the Navy to military contractors; Often jokingly referred to as "Non Mission Capable Internet".

**Non-rate** – Older term meaning junior to the NCO ranks: a Private, Private First Class, or Lance Corporal. This is a derogatory term and will probably not help if you're trying to lead.

**No impact, no idea** – expression denoting a miss on a weapons range (the scorer cannot find an impact on target); also used as an "I don't have any idea" response.

**North Carolina Lawn Dart** - expression denoting the AV-8 and the many mishaps that took place during the aircraft's development and testing.

**NROTC** – Naval Reserve Officer Training Corps, a college-based recruiting program for officers for the Navy and Marine Corps.

# O

**OCONUS** – Outside of CONtinental United States, as opposed to CONUS.

**O-course** – obstacle course.

**OCS** – Officer Candidate School, recruit training for officers.

**O-dark thirty** – very early hours before dawn. Also known as "Zero-Dark Thirty".

**Office hours** – administrative ceremony where legal, disciplinary, and other matters are handled. Pretty much synonymous with NJP these days. Known as Captain's Mast afloat.

**Officers' club or O-Club** – recreation facility for officers that often includes a bar, restaurant, game room, and objects of unit significance, such as old equipment, war trophies; similar to a gentlemen's club.

**Officers' country** – living spaces for officers aboard ship, on a post or station.

**OJT** – On-the-Job Training, sometimes without a formal school or period of instruction, sometimes after a formal school or period of instruction.

**Oki** – Okinawa.

**OMPF** – Official Military Personnel File, a personal record of all awards, punishments, training, and other records on you, compiled and maintained by Headquarters Marine Corps.

**Oorah** or **ooh rah** – spirited cry used since the mid-20th century, comparable to "Hoo-ah" used in the Army or "Hooyah" by Navy SEALs; most commonly used to respond to a verbal greeting or as an expression of enthusiasm and motivation..

**OP** – Observation Post, a position used for reconnaissance.

**Operational tempo** or **optempo** – the pace or speed of operations for a unit or individual.

**OPSEC** – Operation(s/al) Security, counterintelligence efforts to keep generally unclassified but sensitive information (such as troop movements and deployments) from enemies.

**OQR** – Officer Qualification Record, a service record for officers, much like an enlisted Marine's SRB.

**OOB** – Out Of Bounds, or straying into an area restricted from use by normal traffic, prohibited to Marines, or too far from base for a given liberty period.

**OOD** – Officer Of the Day, Officer of the Deck or the senior Marine responsible for the patrol and security of a unit's garrison working spaces and sleeping quarters after working hours, usually responsible for subordinate sentries and acts as a guard commander.

**Oscar Mike** – On the Move, the names of the two NATO phonetic alphabet letters O and M which stand for the phrase. Used on the radio and in shorthand to each other. See also NATO phonetic alphabet.

**OTV** – Outer Tactical Vest, militarized version of Interceptor body armor, a common type of ballistic vest; being replaced by the MTV.

**Overhead** – ceiling.

**Over the hill** – a deserter; someone who leaves the military without being discharged.

**P**

**PALS** – Pouch Attachment Ladder System, a webbing system used to attach combat accessories to MOLLE and ILBE equipment.

**Page 11** – NAVMC 118(11), a page of a Marine's Service Record Book or Officer Qualification Record where administrative remarks are made concerning a Marine's performance and conduct, and which may contain negative recommendations regarding promotion or re-enlistment; while not inherently negative, it is used as a formal counseling tool that becomes part of a Marine's permanent service record and will be reviewed by those making administrative decisions regarding a Marine's career.

**Parade ground/field/deck** – area set aside for the conduct of parades, drill, and ceremonies, often paved or well-maintained lawn.

**Passage-way** – corridor or hallway.

**Passed over** – having failed selection for the next higher rank (for SNCOs and officers).

**Pay grade** – DOD system of designating a U.S. serviceperson's pay (E-1 through E-9, W-1 through W-5, and O-1 through O-10), not to be confused with rank (though the two usually correspond) or billet.

**PCA** – Permanent change of assignment; Remaining in place but chaining from one unit to another.

**PCP** – Physical Conditioning Program, exercise regimen for Marines failing to meet the minimum physical requirements; also Physical Conditioning Platoon, for the unit where a physically unfit recruit is sent prior to recruit training, nicknamed Pork Chop Platoon.

**PCS** – Permanent Change of Station, transfer to another post, station, base, or installation.

**PFC** – Private First Class.

**PFT** – Physical Fitness Test, performance in pull-ups (flexed-arm hang for females), abdominal crunches, and a 3-mile run.

**Phrog** – nickname for CH-46 Sea Knight.

**Phone watch** – duty where a Marine is responsible for answering phones when others are busy or unavailable (such as lunch hours); also used to refer to the person filling the duty.

**PI** – Marine Corps Recruit Depot Parris Island; also "the PI" for the Philippine Islands, a frequent deployment location.

**Pinning or pinning on** – promotion by pinning the new rank insignia onto the MCCUU collar.

**Piss cover or piss cutter** – nickname for soft green garrison cap worn with the service uniform.

**Pit** – depressed area on a shooting range where the targets are located, shooters staff it and mark, raise, and lower targets from behind a berm; also a name for the sand pit Drill Instructors enjoy providing incentive training in.

**Pitting** – incentive training for a large group of recruits, so named for the sandy pits set aside for such events.

**Pizza box** – Marksman Weapons Qualification Badge, so named for its square shape.

**Platoon Sergeant** – SNCO executive to the platoon commander, usually the senior enlisted man.

**PMO** – Provost Marshal's Office, the military police force of a Marine installation.

**Pogue or POG** – Marine not of the combat arms (infantry, armor, and artillery), often used to refer to an Administrative Marine or some other paper-shuffling job.

**Pogey bait** – Candy or sweets.

**Police** – to pick up items (such as litter or expended ammunition casings); to return an area to a natural state; to correct another Marine.

**Poncho liner** – a lightly quilted insulating blanket used to warm the individual wearing a rain poncho, often used as a stand-alone blanket.

**Port** – naval term for "left"; opposite of starboard; Also a nasty, red alcoholic drink served at mess nights.

**Portholes** – military issue eyeglasses, or the wearer of glasses.

**Pot shack** – place in the chow hall where cooking utensils are washed.

**Possible** - slang term for the highest score possible in a marksmanship exercise as in "shooting a possible".

**Prick** – slang for any equipment bearing the "PRC" designator, referring to a Portable Radio Control or man-portable radios.

**Property shed** – place where organizational property is stored, often a warehouse.

**PT** – Physical Training, physical exercise to build or maintain strength, agility, and flexibility.

**Pucker factor** – high level of anxiety experienced by those in dangerous situations.

**Pull butts / pits** – to mark and score targets on a shooting range from behind a berm.

**PX** – Post eXchange, the base store.

## Q

**QRF** – Quick Reaction Force, a highly-mobile stand-by or reserve force designed to add firepower in precise places as the commander decides on a changing battlefield, often used for MEDEVAC purposes.

**Quarter deck** – a location of prominence in a barracks or office; usually close to the entrance.

**Quarter-decking** – incentive training in boot camp by means of repetitive and constant physical exercises, so named because it happens on the Quarter Deck.

**Quarters** – housing, whether bachelor (barracks) or family (government-leased apartments or houses); also the periodic muster of a ship's company.

**Quatrefoil** – four-pointed embroidered pattern stitched on to the top of a Marine officer's barracks cover, from the tradition of wearing it to be identified as friendly to Marine sharpshooters during boarding actions in the era of wooden sailing ships.

# R

**R/S** – Respectfully Submitted, used as an end greeting in written communication.

**Rack** – bed, inappropriate to use the Army term "bunk" except when used in conjunction with "junk on the bunk".

**Radio watch** – duty monitoring radio networks for relevant traffic or simply maintaining those networks; also the person filling that duty.

**Rank Abbreviations**:

| | |
|---|---|
| Private | Pvt |
| Private First Class | PFC |
| Lance Corporal | LCpl |
| Corporal | Cpl |
| Sergeant | Sgt |
| Staff Sergeant | SSgt |
| Gunnery Sergeant | GySgt |
| First Sergeant | 1$^{st}$Sgt |
| Master Sergeant | MSgt |
| Sergeant Major | SgtMaj |
| Master Gunnery Sergeant | MGySgt |
| | |
| Warrant Officer 1 | WO1 |
| Warrant Officer 2 | WO2 |
| Chief Warrant Officer 3 | CWO3 |
| Chief Warrant Officer 4 | CWO4 |
| Chief Warrant Officer 5 | CWO5 |
| | |
| 2$^{nd}$ Lieutenant | 2$^{nd}$Lt |
| 1$^{st}$ Lieutenant | 1$^{st}$Lt |
| Captain | Capt |
| Major | Maj |
| Lieutenant Colonel | LtCol |
| Colonel | Col |
| Brigadier General | BrigGen |
| Major General | MajGen |
| Lieutenant General | LtGen |
| General | Gen |

**Ranks** – there are no acceptable contractions or shortened ways of addressing the following: Private, Lance Corporal, Corporal, Sergeant, Staff Sergeant, Sergeant Major, Warrant Officer/Chief Warrant Officer, Major, Colonel, and General. The following may be addressed informally in the following ways, with permission: Private First Class as PFC, a Gunnery Sergeant as "Gunny", a Master Sergeant as "Top", a Master Gunnery Sergeant as "Master Gunny" or "Master Guns", a Second Lieutenant or First Lieutenant as "Lieutenant", a Captain as "Skipper", and a Brigadier General, Major General, and Lieutenant General as "General". It is inappropriate to abbreviate an enlisted Marine's rank (Sergeant or above) as "Sergeant", "Staff" (for SSgt) or "sarge", as other services sometimes do.

**Ratfuck** – taking parts from one piece of equipment and applying them to another in order to make the receiving equipment usable; A no-no in the maintenance world, sometimes a necessity in the operational world.

**Recon** - used as a verb to denote stealthy acquisition of information. Also, the nickname for Reconnaissance Battalions within each Marine Division.

**Red Patch** – device worn on the uniforms of landing support Marines (usually on the side of each knee and front of the cover) to distinguish the landing support Marines from the Marines landing and moving inland.

**Request mast** – appealing to the commanding officer (or higher if needed, up to the Marines Commanding General) in order to seek satisfaction for a grievance that the requester feels was not adequately corrected at a lower level; USMC orders permit any Marine to request mast up to the individual's commanding general **without repercussions**. That means the NCO's, SNCO's and junior Officers can't make you do extra crap as punishment for filing a request mast. Doing so is a violation of the UCMJ and written USMC orders.

**Re-up** – reenlisting/volunteering for an additional period of service.

**Rotate** – return home at the end of a deployment or period overseas.

**RPGs** – Rocket Propelled Grenades.

**ROE** – Rules Of Engagement are restrictions and guidelines on how and when a Marine may use escalating force on the enemy.

**Running lights** – navigational night lights on a ship.

# S

**SACO** – Substance Abuse Control Officer, a Marine or DOD civilian responsible for the initial screening and evaluation of a Marine or sailor that was shown signs of alcoholism or illegal drug use. The SACO is the CO's direct representative and is authorized to refer Marines and Sailors to the proper medical facilities for rehabilitation & treatment.

**SAFE** – mnemonic for the set up of weapons for a small-units defense, denotes: Security, Automatic weapons, Fields of fire, Entrenchment.

**S/F** – abbreviation for Semper Fidelis when used at the end of a written communication.

**Salty, or salt/salty dog** – experienced or well-worn person or thing.

**Salty language** – profanity.

**SALUTE** – mnemonic device for a situation report (AKA SitRep), denotes: Size, Activity, Location, Unit, Time, and Equipment.

**Sandbox** – Iraq, the middle east in general, or other desert areas.

**SARC** - Sexual Assault Response Coordinator, a Marine (usually an SNCO) assigned as the point of contact for personnel who fall victim to or witness a sexual assault.

**Say again** – request to repeat a statement, question, or order, especially over a radio, or as "I say again" to preface a repetition by the sender; the word "repeat" is not to be used in this context, as it calls for a preceding fire mission to be fired again.

**Schmuckatelli** – generic, unnamed junior Marine, from the Yiddish pejorative "schmuck".

**SCIF** – Sensitive Compartmented Information Facility, a place were classified materials are processed and/or stored.

**Scullery** – place in the chow hall where dishes are washed; sometimes called the "pot shack".

**Scuttlebutt** – gossip, or a drinking fountain. Rumors, and sea stories are also known as scuttlebutt.

**Seabag** or **sea bag** – duffel bag used to carry one's personal belongings. "Duffel bag" is an Army term not used by Marines.

**Seabag drag** – manually carrying personal items (often within seabags) to new or temporary living quarters.

**Sea lawyer** – person who dispenses legal advice based on their limited experience or what they've heard others say. An ignorant idiot.

**Sea story** – story, tale, or yarn used to impress others; sometimes contains exaggeration or even outright lies.

**Second award** - used in conjunction with awards, but also denotes achieving a rank for the second time after being previously busted as in "Lance Corporal - Second Award".

**Secret squirrel** – intelligence or agency personnel or activities.

**Secure** – stop, cease; or to put away and/or lock up.

**Semper Fi** – shortened version of "Semper Fidelis", the motto of the Corps, Latin for "always faithful".

**Semper Gumby** - colloquialism denoting tactical flexibility and the ability to quickly adapt to changing circumstances.

**Semper I** – colloquialism denoting selfish or self-centered behavior.

**Ships Company** – a platoon of Marines charged with contributing to the operation of a ship while afloat; usually involves mess duty, guard duty and/or manning small arms.

**Shit bag** or **shit bird** – a habitually unkempt or undisciplined Marine.

**Shit-Hot** - term used to identify something or someone as exceptional or very good. Not to be confused with Hot-Shit.

**Shitter** – bathroom or head; also a nickname for the CH-53 helicopter because of the trail of grey exhaust it leaves while in flight.

**Shooter** – person whose primary duty involves marksmanship with a rifle or pistol, such as Marines at the rifle range or shooting team members.

**Shore party** – landing support specialists that direct the disposition of troops and equipment during an amphibious assault or a deployment landing.

**Short-timer** – person nearing the completion of his/her present tour of duty or enlistment.

**Short-timer's disease** – apathy to duties and regulations from a person nearing EAS.

**Shove off** – to leave the vicinity, from the naval term meaning to push a boat off the shore or pier.

**Shower shoes** – pair of rubber sandals issued to recruits to prevent the spread of infections from the use of community or shared showers.

**Sick bay** – infirmary or other medical facility aboard ship, also refers to Battalion Aid Stations (BAS) and medical offices ashore.

**Sick call** – daily period (usually first thing in the morning) when routine ailments are treated at sick bay.

**Sick call commando** – person who constantly finds reasons to go to medical; implies some is a hypochondriac or malingerer; sometimes associated with "laminated light duty chit".

**Side arms** – weapon (usually a pistol) carried by a sentry under arms.

**Side straddle hop** – a "Jumping Jack".

**Sight in** – aim a weapon at a target using the sights, considered an intention to shoot the target.

**Silver bullet** – rectal thermometer used to check the core temperature of a person suffering from heat-related injuries, such as hyperthermia, heat exhaustion and heat stroke.

**Skate** – avoiding work by finding an excuse to be elsewhere or unavailable; also used as an adjective to describe an easier duty.

**Skid squadron** – Marine Light Attack Helicopter Squadron, so named because the AH-1 SuperCobra and UH-1N Huey helicopters have skids instead of wheels for landing gear.

**Skivvies** – a traditional but ridiculous name for underwear: skivvie shirt (T-shirt) and skivvie drawers (underwear).

**Skylark** – to casually frolic or take excess time to complete a task. In 20 years as a Marine, I never had the opportunity to "casually frolic" anywhere.

**Slick sleeves** – this is what NCO's use to call me when I was a private; refers to the fact that a person does not wear any rank insignia (an E-1).

**Slide bite** – a pinch or abrasion of the hand due to holding a semi-automatic pistol too close to the recoiling slide.

**SMEAC** – mnemonic for the five paragraph order, a method of clearly issuing complex orders; denotes: Situation, Mission, Execution, Administration & Logistics, Command & Signal.

**Smokey Bear** – brown campaign cover worn by drill instructors, so named because of their similarity to the hat worn by Smokey Bear. See also campaign cover, field hat, & hat.

**Smokin' and jokin'** – a group of Marines sitting around, smoking and talking.

**SNAFU** – Situation Normal, All Fouled/Fucked Up.

**SNCOIC** – Staff Non-Commissioned Officer In Charge, a SNCO responsible for a group of Marines, but without the authority of a commissioned officer; also NCOIC.

**Snap in** – conduct sighting in or aiming exercises with an unloaded weapon.

**Snow job** – a misleading or grossly exaggerated report.

**Snuffie** or **snuffy** – another stupid, derogatory name for a junior Marine, usually a Lance Corporal or below.

**SOP** – Standard Operating Procedure, the routine manner of handling a set situation, can be a standing order.

**SOS** – international distress signal; or Shit On a Shingle, creamed beef on toast, a chow hall specialty that I managed to avoid for 20 years.

**SOTG** – Special Operations Training Group

**Spit and polish** – extreme individual or collective military neatness; from spit-polishing boots and dress shoes.

**Spit-shine** – polish leather footwear (boots and dress shoes), employing spit to help produce a highly polished shine.

**Squadbay** – Nearly extinct now, but living quarters with large open rooms and a shared head.

**Square(d) away** – make neat and regulation appearance, to be in a neat and regulation appearance. See also, un-fuck.

**Squid** – derogatory term for a sailor.

**SRB** – Service Record Book, an administrative record of an enlisted Marine's personal information, promotions, postings, deployments, punishments, and emergency data.

**Staff NCO** or **SNCO** – Staff NonCommissioned Officer; Marines in the rank of E-6 to E-9: Staff Sergeant, Gunnery Sergeant, Master Sergeant, First Sergeant, Master Gunnery Sergeant and Sergeant Major.

**Stand by** – wait, stop and wait (on the ground); continue and wait (in the air).

**Starboard** – naval term for "right", opposite of port.

**STOL** – Short TakeOff/Landing, takeoff and landing technique needing only a short runway to become airborne.

**STOVL** – Short TakeOff, Vertical Landing, takeoff and landing technique where a V/STOL aircraft can make a non-vertical take-off to carry greater weight, such as fuel and weapons, expend that weight, and make a vertical landing. Usually conducted by AV-8's and V-22's.

**Survey** – to trade in an item of government property for a new one, by reason of un-serviceability (no longer useful).

**Susie Rotten-crotch** – name referring to wife, girlfriends, or other generic women that young men associated with before entering boot camp.

**Swab** – mop; also pejorative for sailor.

**Swamp-ass** – the unpleasant feeling of sweat soaked undergarments.

**Swinging dick** – vulgarity for a male Marine; usually used to emphasize an order to a whole group instead of an individual.

# T

**TAD** – Temporary Assigned Duty, a duty where the Marine or Sailor is detached from his or her unit temporarily and serves elsewhere; comparable to the Army term TDY.

**TBS** – The Basic School, the six month combat training school for new Marine officers.

**Terminal lance** – Marine lance corporal that is unlikely to get promoted before EAS'ing; also a hilarious comic strip of the same name found on the internet and published in the Marine Corps Times.

**The Rock** – Okinawa.

**Thousand yard stare** – unfocused gaze of a battle-weary Marine.

**Tie-ties** – straps or strings used to tie items to another line, such as rifle targets.

**Tip of the spear** – term for a unit or subunit that typically enters enemy territory first.

**T/O&E** – Table of Operations and Equipment, a list authorizing a unit personnel of a particular rank and MOS, as well as organic equipment; often seen separately as T/O and T/E.

**Top** – informal nickname for a Master Sergeant, inappropriate to use without permission.

**Topside** – ship's upper deck.

**Tore up** – broken, messy, unserviceable.

**TRAM** – Tractor, Rubber-tired, Articulated steering, Multi-purpose; heavy lift tractor usually used with Conex style shipping containers.

**T-rats** – Tray ration, nickname for Unitized Group Ration, a ration heated and served to a group of service members; essentially, a bulk form of MRE.

**Two-block** – hoist a flag or pennant to the peak, truck, or yardarm of a staff; or a tie with the knot positioned exactly in the gap of a collar of a buttoned shirt.

# U

**UA** – Unauthorized Absence, the naval version of the term AWOL.

**UAS** – Unmanned Aerial System.

**UAV** – Unmanned Aerial Vehicle.

**UCMJ** – Uniform Code of Military Justice (Public Law 506, 81st Congress) 1951, the system of military law, both judicial and non-judicial.

**UD** – Unit Diary, a computerized system that is used to maintain all administrative records for a unit and its Marines.

**Un-fuck** – to correct some deficiency.

**Under arms** – status of having a weapon, sidearm, "MP" or "SP" brassard, or wearing equipment pertaining to an arm such as a sword sling, pistol belt, or cartridge belt as part of guard duty; Marines under arms do not remove covers indoors.

**Under way** – to depart or to start a process for an objective.

**Unq** – pronounced "U-N-K", unqualified, usually in reference to training events such as the Rifle Range. Going Unq on the range makes you non-promotable, so don't do that.

**Unsat** – abbreviation of unsatisfactory.

**USMC** – Acronym for United States Marine Corps. Also twisted into other acronyms like: Uncle Sam's Misguided Children, U Signed the Mother-fucking Contract (a personal favorite), Uncomplicated Shit Made Complicated.

**USO** – United Service Organization; nonprofit organization that provides morale and recreational services to members of the U.S. military worldwide.

**Utilities** – field and work uniforms, also known as "Cammies" and "Digi's" for the pixilated, digital look of the current uniform; sometimes referred to as the Army term "BDU" (Battle Dress Uniform) by people who have no idea what they're talking about.

# V

**VERTREP** – vertical replenishment, the use of helicopters for cargo transfer to ships or distant outposts.

**VTOL** – Vertical TakeOff/Landing, takeoff and landing technique that does not need a runway to become airborne. See also STOL, STOVL, & V/STOL.

**V/STOL** – Vertical/Short Takeoff and Landing, a type of aircraft that can perform STOL, STOVL, and VTOL.

**W**

**War belt** – a web belt used to carry canteens, ammo pouches and other miscellaneous equipment.

**War paint** – camouflage face paint.

**Watch** – formal tour of duty of prescribed length, usually a guard-related task.

**Water buffalo** or **water bull** – 400-gallon potable water tank, trailer-mounted, towed behind a truck. These are very common water sources on Marine installations (in garrison) and on deployment.

**Wet down** – celebration in honor of a Marines promotion as an officer or in the SNCO ranks, so named for the tradition of wetting the promotion warrant, usually with an alcoholic beverage.

**Whiskey locker** — supply locker/closet.

**Whites** – Marine Corps or Navy white dress uniforms; tends to come in and out of style. As of 2012 white are an Officer and SNCO uniform only..

**WP** or **Willie Pete** – White Phosphorus munitions, whether in grenade, mortar, artillery, or aerial bomb form, so named from the pre-1956 phonetic alphabet letters "William" and "Peter"; now called "Whiskey Pappa".

**Wilco** – voice radio term shortened from "Will Comply".

**Willie peter bag** – a waterproof bag, organizationally issued.

**Winger** – any Marine who serves in the Air Wing, whether a pilot, mechanic or aviation supply.

**Wire** – defensive perimeter of a firm base usually identified as several strands of concertina wire (razor or barbed wire) or a fence-line, crossing it denotes the end of relative safety.

**Wooly pully** – green wool sweater worn with the service uniform (or blue with the dress uniform) over the khaki shirt.

**Word** – general term for instructions, orders, and information that is required for all members of a unit to know; or the act of passing information to a collected group of Marines. See also gouge.

**WM** – an offensive term for a Woman Marine. Inappropriate to use.

**X**

Can't think of much for X, but crossing your forearms over your head in front of a moving aircraft signals the pilot to stop.

# Y

**Yellow leg** – Marine, nickname given by North Korean Army in reference to Korean War-era discolored, yellow-looking leggings.

**Yut** – exclamation of enthusiasm or approval, similar to "oorah" but not as accepted.

# Z

**Zero** - pronounced "zee-row" in an exaggerated manner, as used by Drill Instructors at the end of a count-down implying that recruits are to immediately cease all activity and remain silently in place; also refers to an officer, referring to the O in front of their rank designation, as in O-4.

**Zero-dark thirty** – a really early time for which personnel are required to assemble for an activity, or just an early time of morning before the sun comes up.

**Zoomie** – An Air Force pilot, or any Air Force person.

**Zulu** – A common time reference in which times are give as current time in the **Z** time zone (on the prime meridian). Zulu time is what we Marines use operationally; also known as UTC or Universal Coordinated Time (no, that's not a typo).

# ABOUT THE AUTHOR

MSgt D. Gowans was an active duty Marine for over 20 years. During his career he's worked in both ground side and wing side MOS's, served in numerous billets and participated in numerous deployments. MSgt Gowans is now retired and lives abroad.

Made in the USA
Charleston, SC
02 May 2013